Growing Up ME

A guide to scrapbooking childhood stories

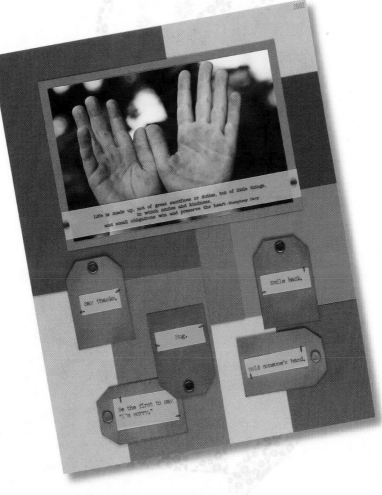

by Angie Pedersen

FORE-WORD(S)

Dedication. To my children, James and Joanne, who have so many stories to tell.

To my husband David, for patiently listening to all of their stories as well as mine.

Acknowledgements. Heartfelt thanks to my parents and my in-laws for babysitting while I finished this book; the Kroppin' Kids and Denise Perkins-Fields from Magical Memories, Verona Island, Maine, for their layouts and feedback on rough drafts; CanTeach.ca, Merle O'Brien and David Kellin for use of their journaling prompts; Jean Bergenson and Melissa Okonski for their support and words of encouragement; the Babes and my Yahoo Groups lists for their unfailing support and cheerleading; all my layout and quote contributors; and finally, Elaine Floyd, who turns my words into a work of art.

Cover credits. "Friends" lettering is by Debra Beagle; "Friends" layout is by Angie Pedersen. "Be Your Own Kind Beautiful" layout is by Barbara LeHoullier. "Share" is by Jessie Baldwin. Title page layout is "Kindness" by Annie Wheatcraft.

First Edition. Printed and bound in the USA
08 07 06 05 04　　5 4 3 2 1

Library of Congress Control Number: 2003114676

ISBN: 1-930500-15-7

Published by:
EFG, Inc.; (314) 762-9762

Distributed to the trade by:
North Light Books
an imprint of F&W Publications, Inc.
4700 East Galbraith Road
Cincinnati, OH 45236
fax: (513) 531-4082
tel: (800) 289-0963

Scrapbooking benefits children in many different ways. Here are some insights on scrapbooking from parents, craft experts, writers and educators.

Creative Expression. Creativity expert and author Tera Leigh believes, "Creativity gives us our voice…children are surrounded by so many rules. Creativity has no rules; through it we are often able to explore our true feelings without fear of being told we have done it wrong. In addition, storytelling encourages children to pay attention to the details of their day so they can later report their observations in their journaling."

Written Expression. For the daughter of Joanne Spouse-Nastasi, "Scrapbooking at school has helped her with story writing and composition. She is more aware of sentence structure and is reading books at a higher level than I expected for her age."

Family Bonds. Elementary school teacher Diana Scott suggests that, "Scrapbooking can help your child become closer to family by remembering holidays, vacations and other special family moments. They might forget a lot of special times with their families and not realize what their unique role in the family is."

Stronger Self-Esteem. Scrapbook instructor Missy Jennings uses scrapbooking with her eight-year-old stepdaughter to build her sense of self. "She is so proud of her pages. They make her feel good. They make her feel like she's good at something, and that means she can be good at other things, too. "

Children need to believe they are good. They need to know that what they think, want and hope for is worthwhile and attainable.

Physical, Social and Emotional Skills. Early Childhood Educator Dana McCabe says, "Scrapbooking can help children develop their fine motor skills with cutting, writing, stamping and punching with precision and neatness. Scrapbooking can be a very social activity and can encourage children to work together, share tools and ideas, ask questions or ask for help.

"Scrapbooking can help children deal with emotions that are unfamiliar to them. They can work through something that is upsetting them, whether it be a death in the family or the loss of a pet. It can also help them express emotions that are uncomfortable for them to express openly such as love, friendship, gratitude and joy."

Organization and Planning Skills. McCabe sees scrapbooking as a way for children to consider the process of art. "It is the whole of creating a page or album. What goes into this? What do I want to say? What do I want this to look like when I'm done? They can dream and plan, they can express their hopes and fears, and they can work with others to accomplish all of this."

Looking Ahead. Scrapbooking allows children to plan for that future. High school art teacher Missy Fortenberry reports, "My older students seem to realize that what's happening now is helping shape them into the adults that they will be tomorrow. Scrapbooking also allows children to plan for that future."

CONTENTS:

WELCOME

You spend countless hours with the children in your life—you could probably scrap many of these stories yourself. In fact, I know many times you have.

But it will mean more coming from them, whether you use their words for the journaling on a layout you've done or they scrap the whole layout themselves.

Their stories will be captured in their own voices, which illustrates their perspective, priorities and sense of humor. It will also mean more to your child, since he or she will have created something. Include your child in the process and he or she will feel a sense of ownership, as well as the sense that you will listen when there is a story to share.

I am a Puzzle
by Angie Pedersen

Just for fun, before we get into the projects and roles in *Growing Up ME*, I wanted to tell you more about myself so you have a better feel for this book.

SUPPLIES: Patterned paper is by DMD Industries, Hot Off the Press, Creative Imaginations, K&Co, 7Gypsies and Wordsworth. Charms are by Westrim. Clearly Creative Transparency is from Scrappy's. Title fonts are Gigi ("I am a") and MA Sexy ("Puzzle"). Journaling font is Century Gothic. Brown ink is by Ranger Inks.

When I started working on my Book of Me scrapbook, my kids, then ages seven and four, asked me when they could start working on their Book of Me.

I started working with my oldest child James first. We dug out his baby pictures and took pictures of him reading his favorite book. I expected that together we would create pretty typical "this is me as a baby and this is when I was born" pages.

What I didn't expect was how little help he would need (or want!) from me. What I didn't expect was his own ideas for how the pages should look and for future pages he could do ("I could do a page on that!") And what I didn't expect was how close I would feel to him, sharing this hobby together.

I also didn't anticipate what a wonderful teaching tool this project could be. As an education major, I soon realized that many different skills go into the creation of a scrapbook layout. As he worked, James was drawing upon elements of art, language, math, fine motor development and problem solving.

James also experienced a strong sense of self-esteem upon seeing his completed work. I got such a kick out of watching him work and thought more childen should have the opportunity to experience this.

I am a Puzzle

PARIS

"Just go with it."

"It takes courage to grow up and be who you really are."
-e.e. cummings

spirit soul essence

puzzle
\Puzzle\. n.
1. Something which perplexes; especially, a toy or a problem that requires ingenuity and often persistence in solving or assembling; something exhibiting marvelous skill in making.

I am a puzzle
Not all of my pieces are the same size.
Nor do they fit together smoothly
But I need every one of my pieces
Everything I learn
Every person I meet
Every challenge I face
Everything I experience
Adds another piece to the puzzle
Only these pieces create
The Puzzle of Me

"Exactly what I want."   "I am what I am."

I wanted other children to be able to share and preserve the stories of their lives, told from their perspective. I wanted them to feel that their stories are worth telling and for them to get excited about illustrating them with a scrapbook. I wanted to give parents and educators the tools to be able to confidently guide children through this process. So *Growing Up ME* was born.

Who can use *Growing Up ME*?

In this book, I'll guide you in working with children to create a scrapbook about themselves. This book is for parents, children, teachers, scout leaders, social workers, Sunday School teachers, foster care workers and counselors.

If you have children or work with children, you can make a difference by encouraging them to tell their stories. The ideas and journaling prompts offered in *Growing Up ME* encourage children to explore what is unique and special about themselves. You can also use this book to create Book of Me pages about your own childhood.

When working with children, you can act as a cheerleader. You're there to say, "You can *do* this. What you say matters." You can support children in the process of defining the stories they want to tell and how to get the full story on the page. In the time you spend together, you can point out things that might be worth scrapping.

Introducing Kids to Scrapbooking

I have compiled some tips on introducing scrapbooking to children. You can find them at www.scrapyourstories.com/kidstarters.htm.

I am a Puzzle
by James Pedersen

My son James has contributed many of his ideas and layouts to this book. I thought you may want to meet him here, too!

SUPPLIES: Paper is by Paper Patch. Paper doll is by EK Success. Letter stickers are by Provo Craft.

How to use *Growing Up ME*

Growing Up ME is different from other layout idea books because it encourages a team-approach to scrapbooking with children. The journaling prompts also encourage children to include more meaningful journaling so friends and family get a better sense of the scrapper as a person. Many kids like to do layouts on what they do and where they've been, rather than who they are as a person. *Growing Up ME* can help add meaning to children's scrapbooks.

This book is designed it to appeal to a variety of audiences. Here are some ways to approach the ideas:

1. Look through the prompts and layout examples, choose a topic, and present it to a child in your life: "Would you like to do a page on ...?"

2. Choose five to 10 different prompts and list them on a worksheet. Have your child answer them in journal entries.

3. Let your child look through the book, choose his or her own topic, and just be present for help or questions.

4. Use the chapters to provide theme ideas for a series of activities with children—one session on Friendship, another session on Family, another session on Teamwork. One activity could be a scrapbook layout, but you could also encourage bookmarks, letters, cards or a frameable gift. Use the prompts and ideas to guide each session.

5. Use these ideas as the basis for pages about the children in your life. You scrap the page, and then turn to them to get the journaling in their words.

Having It Their Way
by Libby Weifenbach

Note how Libby's layout is different from her daughter's, shown on the next page. Libby's design shows a sense of balance and grid. The journaling is told from her perspective—she doesn't mention her daughter's "injury," even though it was memorable to Kendra. Note how, while people may experience the same event, their experiences won't be the same. Kids have their own stories to tell!

SUPPLIES: Patterned paper is by KI Memories. Cardstock is by Bazzill Basics. Stickers are by Creative Imaginations ("Having it" and "Way"), Wordsworth ("Their") and Doodlebug ("Burger King"). Stamp ("at") is by PSX Designs, Diamond glaze and double mats are by Scrapbook Wizard.

6. Many of the prompts and layout ideas can be applied to your own childhood memories. Take time to scrap you too! (See *The Book of ME: A guide to scrapbooking about yourself* for more ideas.)

Ready to be inspired?

Growing Up ME focuses on what I call the "positives" in your child's life. It's about preserving the stories of childhood and all the things that make them unique. It's about celebrating what makes each child shine. It is independent of age, native language, religion and family structure. Every child is unique and every child has stories to tell. It's time to get them told.

Angie

Burger King Fun
by Kendra Weifenbach, age 6

Kendra wanted to record all of the fun she had on one of the first warm days of spring. Her journaling describes all of her favorite parts of the afternoon, plus a couple of "low" points. While she uses the same pictures as her mom, Kendra's journaling tells the story from her perspective, detailing everything that is most important to her. Her mother's layout tells a different story…

SUPPLIES: Title stickers are by Making Memories. Line stickers are by Mrs. Grossman's. Die cut "fun" is by Cut-It-Up. Frames are by Memories Forever. Font is CK Handprint. Decorative edge scissors are by Fiskars.

This is the day we went to Burger King. It was fun going down the slide. We (Taylor and Kendra) were playing tag and hide & seek. My favorite part was seeing the roof when I climbed up really high. I got stuck up in the high square, and Taylor had to come get me down. I really like eating at Burger King because they give fun toys. My brother opened the door, and it scratched my foot. It hurt a little.

AUTHOR'S NOTE:
Libby and Kendra Weifenbach, whose pages appears here, are among the 37 different scrapbookers who contributed to this book. You'll see the work of the others who graciously gave their permission to use their layouts in the coming chapters.

1: My Beginnings

This section encourages children to look back at their younger selves and see their own beginnings, charting a way through "baby milestones."

Kids love to hear stories about themselves. My son frequently asks me, "What was I like as a baby?" My daughter loves to hear that we called her "monkey" because she climbed on everything. Think of the fun page she could do with these stories!

Explore what the world was like at the time of birth and how the family prepared for the child's arrival. Children can document feelings about their names and see what famous people share their name and birthday. Explore past birthdays, reminding children that every year there's a celebration just to honor the fact they're alive.

Suggest that your child approach family members or friends to get stories about his or her early years. Use the forms on the book at scrapyourstories.com/forms.htm to collect favorite memories. This reinforces to your child that other people have been involved in following his or her life for longer than perhaps realized.

Make color copies of the responses so you can have a sample of the handwriting of friends and family in your child's scrapbook. Or, you could suggest family and friends use a photo-safe pen and have them record their memories on acid-free paper to include in the scrapbook.

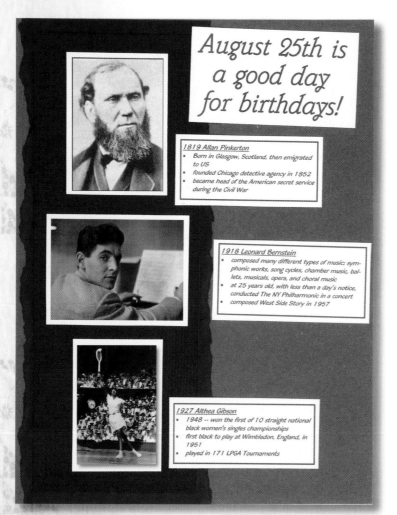

August 25th is a good day for birthdays!

1819 Allan Pinkerton
• Born in Glasgow, Scotland, then emigrated to US
• founded Chicago detective agency in 1852
• became head of the American secret service during the Civil War

1918 Leonard Bernstein
• composed many different types of music: symphonic works, song cycles, chamber music, ballets, musicals, opera, and choral music
• at 25 years old, with less than a day's notice, conducted The NY Philharmonic in a concert
• composed West Side Story in 1957

1927 Althea Gibson
• 1948 -- won the first of 10 straight national black women's singles championships
• first black to play at Wimbledon, England, in 1951
• played in 171 LPGA Tournaments

August 25th
by Angie Pedersen

To do this page, I went to www.historyorb.com (see links) for a list of people born on my birthday. I also used the Internet to find three facts about each person along with a photo. It was interesting to see who was born on this day.

Supplies: Paper is cardstock. Title font is Belwe Mono Italic; journaling font is Blacklight.

Why is this theme important?

Children love to see pictures of themselves as babies. It reinforces how far they've come and how big they are now. They love to share these pictures with friends and a scrapbook is the perfect place to do this. Learning more about their birth—and the preparations for that birth allows them to see how wanted they were by their families. Learning more about their names helps give them a feeling of connection to their families and to other people who share their names.

There may be situations where children do not have pictures or stories of their early childhood. (Many adults scrapbooking their childhoods have this challenge, too.) Instead, consider creating pages on what was going on in the world at the time of their birth, pages with poems using their name, or pages with historical data for the city in which they were born.

Be creative in suggesting topics for children in unusual situations. Don't focus on the negative or missing aspects of their lives. Encourage children to see themselves as special and unique.

In my children's scrapbooks...

My son did a page of various baby pictures. He included journaling about what baby foods he disliked and other funny incidents. He also did a page of historical information found at online dMarie's Time Capsule (see Internet Resources on page 13). My daughter wants to do a page of funny baby faces she made and pictures of her climbing on all our furniture (a page most likely decorated with monkeys).

We find delight in the beauty and happiness of children that makes the heart too big for the body.

—Ralph Waldo Emerson

A birthday is a time to plan ahead and to dream of all the beautiful things that life has to offer.

—Unknown

Most of us can remember a time when a birthday—especially if it was one's own—brightened the world as if a second sun had risen.

—Robert Lynd

Natasha Sarah Yaceyko

by Natasha Yaceyko, age 16

Children often like to start their books with a baby page. Use baby photos and include details like Natasha did— list parents, birthdate, time of birth, weight, doctor, hospital and location.

Supplies: Heart punch by Family Treasures. Dots added and dotted printing used in title.

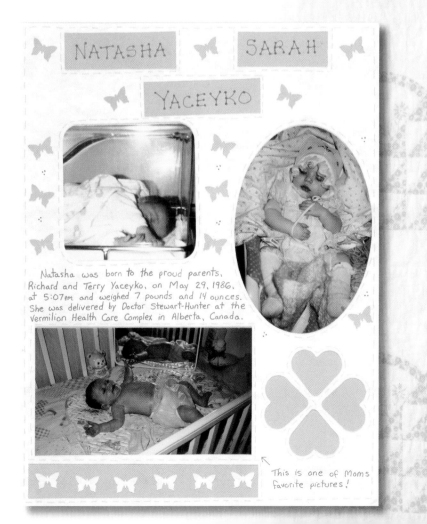

Natasha was born to the proud parents, Richard and Terry Yaceyko, on May 29, 1986, at 5:07pm and weighed 7 pounds and 14 ounces. She was delivered by Doctor Stewart-Hunter at the Vermilion Health Care Complex in Alberta, Canada.

This is one of Moms favorite pictures!

Birthdays are ordinary days sprinkled with stardust.
—Unknown

Birthdays give us opportunities to stop and appreciate all the beautiful things we have been blessed with.
—Unknown

It is important to honor our beginnings. It is important to remember that we matter and that we have a place in this world that no one else has.
—Hallmark greeting card

Prompts to trigger journaling

❏ Talk about your birth. Where, when and what events surrounded your birth? Who was waiting for you to be born?

❏ What were your baby milestones? Did you approach rolling over, smiling, crawling, walking, talking, first tooth or solid foods in a unique way?

❏ When is your birthday? Do any famous people share your birthday? Name three facts about three famous people who share your birthday.

❏ Name three historical events that happened on your birthday (not necessarily your birth year).

❏ Make a "Timeline of Me." List important dates or events, from birth to present-day. Feel free to illustrate with related photos or drawings.

❏ Tell one of your favorite stories of you as a young child. Which stories do your parents tell over and over about you? What are some funny things you did as a baby or young child? Have a parent write one of the stories to include in your scrapbook.

❏ Describe your best birthday party or your favorite birthday present. Draw a picture of it.

❏ If you could have your favorite dinner for your birthday, what would it be?

❏ Research historical data for the year you were born. Who was President? Who won the Academy Awards? How much did a gallon of milk cost? Gasoline?

MY NAME

Jazzy Spirit
American Life

Messy Hair

Energetic Soul

Scrappy my pet hamster

8 years old 2002

My Name
by James Pedersen, age 8

Part of the fun of scrapbook journaling is experimenting with different techniques. An arostic poem is a poem that uses the letters of a word to begin each line. First, write a name or word down the page vertically. On each line, write a word or phrase starting with the same letter.

While this example isn't exactly a poem, James uses the arostic technique to describe himself. This piece could be adapted into a full poem or could include photos that illustrate each descriptive term.

SUPPLIES: Paper is by Sonburn.

- ❑ Look at trends from that date. What was "hot" and what was not? What was going on in the world? Use the dMarie Time Capsule or other related Internet Resources to gather this information online (see the Web resources at the end of this chapter).

- ❑ What is your full name? Why did your parents choose your name? Were you named after anyone? Do you like your name? Have you ever wished you could change it? What name would you chose?

- ❑ What famous people share your first name? Name three facts about three famous people who share your name.

- ❑ Research the meaning of your name. Do you think the meaning is right for you?

- ❑ Do you have any nicknames? Who gave them to you?

- ❑ How do you think your parents would describe you as a baby? How would your sibling(s) describe the baby you were? Ask them to write down their thoughts or memories to include in your book.

- ❑ Create an acrostic poem using the letters in your name (see Web resources).

- ❑ Create a bio-poem using your name (see Web resources).

Don't forget that compared to a grownup person every baby is a genius.

—May Sarton

A new baby is like the beginning of all things—wonder, hope and a dream of possibilities.

—Eda J. Le Shan

For a child, each new day brings so many new exciting things.

—Unknown

Sleepover Birthday Party
by Kennedy Wools, 8

Kennedy's birthday layout includes all of the essentials—pictures of the party, a list of the guests and a description of the party activities. All of these things will help her remember the fun she had at her party.

SUPPLIES: Paper is by Paper Patch. Stickers are by Me & My Big Ideas

I can see the fingerprints of God when I look at you. Never has there been and never again will there be another you.
—Stephen Curtis Chapman

I have no special gift. I am only passionately curious.
—Albert Einstein

It is not a slight thing when those so fresh from God love us.
—Charles Dickens

Tell me, is there any part of me that is not lovable?
—Tzu Tzu Yeh

When the first baby laughed for the first time, the laugh broke into a thousand pieces and they all went skipping about, and that was the beginning of fairies.
—James M. Barrie

Who can gaze at a newborn baby, and not wonder again at the miracle?
—Pearl S Buck

A name is what a man makes it. My father did well with his, and I hope to do the same.
—Louis L'Amour

A child sings before it speaks, dances almost before it walks…music is with us from the beginning.
—Pamela Brown

The beginnings of all things are small.
—Cicero

❑ What are or were your favorite toys?

❑ Did/do you have a favorite blanket or stuffed animal? Did/do you have a name for it? What did/do you like to do with it?

❑ What games did you play as a young child—inside and outside?

❑ Did you have a hide-out or secret place when you were younger? Where? Describe it and draw a picture of it.

Photos to find or request

❑ Picture of mom pregnant with child

❑ Picture of the person your child is named after

❑ Picture of a birthday party

❑ Pictures of "baby milestones": rolling over, smiling, crawling, walking, talking, first tooth, solid foods, etc.

❑ Baby gifts given around the time of birth (include journaling on who gave each gift)

Pictures to take

❑ Picture of favorite baby toys

❑ Picture of baby blanket

❑ Internet photos of famous people that share his or her name or birthday

❑ Internet photo of the President the year he or she was born

dMarie Time Capsule
by James Pedersen, age 8 assisted by Angie Pedersen

The dMarie Time Capsule is a great way to get a "snapshot" of American life on a specific date. This printout showcases information from the time James was born. He surfed the Internet for pictures to highlight some of the noteworthy items. Consider looking through covers of major magazines to give a taste of current events. Most magazines have a Website and some archives feature archives of past covers.

SUPPLIES: Patterned paper is by Keeping Memories Alive. Decorative scissors are by Fiskars. Information sheet from www.dmarie.com/timecap; "Friends" cover graphic from www.rollingstone.com/photos/default.asp.

Famous Angie's
by Angie Pedersen

This layout is based on a design from page 92 of Stacy Julian's book, *Simple Scrapbooks*. To do this page, I went to www.imdb.com and searched for my first name. I found historical information at the site and pulled journal entries for each person on my layout. I also included some personal information like how I used to watch the TV show or where I heard the song.

SUPPLIES: Patterned paper is by ProvoCraft. Title font is Bongo Fraktur; journaling font is Blacklight. Images downloaded from the Internet.

Brady Means... *by Brady MacLeod, age 7*

Brady included three different name activites on this layout—an acrostic poem using his name, a printout of the meaning of his name and a bio-poem about himself. Brady also included a baby photo along with a current photo. This layout provides a quick snapshot of Brady at age 7.

SUPPLIES: Font is Comic Sans. Hand lettering by Brady. The meaning of Brady was downloaded from www.namestusa.com.

www.

The meaning of your name:
www.enlightenedsoftware.com/babynames/

Famous names:
jas.family.go.com/babynamer?page=SearchForm

Famous birthdays:
us.imdb.com/onthisday
www.famousbirthdays.com/

Historical data from the year you were born:
dmarie.com/timecap

Historical events on your birthday:
www.historychannel.com/tdih/

Bio-poem lesson plan:
www.studyguide.org/bio%20poem%20assignment.htm
www.askeric.org/cgi-bin/printlessons.cgi/Virtual/Lessons/Language_Arts/Writing/WCP0003.html

Fonts for kids:
www.momscorner4kids.com/fonts/index.htm

Write an autobiography:
www.inspired2write.com/wordweav/lifelore/lifelo0.html

Autobiographical scrapbook project:
www.oldfashionedliving.com/biography.html

2: MY FAMILY

This section explores your child's family and community relationships. These can be the people he or she lives with as well as the place in which he or she lives.

Family is such a basic component of a person's life. Family forms the basis of many of your child's beliefs, behaviors and decisions.

Pediatrician Marianne Neifert writes, "The family... represents a child's initial source of unconditional love and acceptance and provides lifelong connectedness with others. A family is where a child learns to display affection, control his temper and pick up his toys. Finally, a family is a perpetual source of encouragement, advocacy, assurance, and emotional refueling that empowers a child to venture with confidence into the greater world and to become all that he can be."

Why is this theme important?

Children form perspectives on what the word "family" means based on who they live with. A family may mean both parents, one parent, grandparents, foster parents or some other situation. Children need a place to explore their familial relationships and to affirm for themselves what they like best about each family member (even though they may deny ever actually *liking* a sibling!)

Creating pages about "family" in a scrapbook will help your child define himself or herself in relation to a family unit, as well as considering their ideals for family life. These explorations will help them see the

share

traditions they want to preserve when they start their own families.

Scrapbooks can provide children with a place to preserve memories of things they've done with their families, reminding them of the happy times spent together, whether at Grandma's house, at the zoo or on a camping trip. Looking back on time spent with family reminds your child that they are part of a group and this fosters a sense of belonging.

For teachers, leaders and social workers, if you work with a child with an atypical family situation or if some of the following prompts bring up unpleasant memories, try to shift the focus to more "superficial" topics, like drawing a picture of their house or room, telling a funny story about a family member, a family pet or the family they'd like to have when they grow up.

You can also bypass this section entirely—all of the prompts and ideas offered in this book are just suggestions. Tailor the project to work best for your situation, and bring out the best in the child at your side.

In my children's scrapbooks...

My son chose to do pages mostly on funny incidents (now why would a nine-year-old choose to do pages that might embarrass his parents?), as well as some pages on family trips to the lake during the summer. My daughter drew pictures of each of us and dictated what she likes best about each person.

A mother's arms are made of tenderness and children sleep soundly in them.
—Victor Hugo

We cannot all do great things, but we can all do small things with great love.
—Mother Theresa

"Love isn't eternal; it's day to day. It brings home the bacon and fries it. It wipes noses. It makes the bed. Sometimes it even yells."
—Joseph Sobran

There are advantages of being the firstborn in a family, one of which was the fact that I was an only child for two years. I was the only one my parents had to look after, the only one who would entertain them, the only one who got the attention of the grandparents. Then my sister Melinda came along, and everything changed. Of course it was exciting to have a little sister at first. She was a cute little bald baby. But then the novelty of a baby wore off and I am sure I asked my mom to send her back. Especially when she got older and learned to take things. What do you mean, I have to share? Those are MY toys!! That's MY room! Wait, is that my favorite sweater? I don't care that it doesn't fit me anymore! I don't want HER to wear it! Thoughts such as these were verbalized on a daily basis. However, about the time this picture was taken (1978 – I was 3, Melinda was 1), I became acutely aware of something. I had a little sister – a playmate who never had to go home. Someone who would keep me company no matter what. And, I realized, someone who looked up to me – who admired me and wanted to be like me. Sure, she was irritating a lot of the time, and there were still plenty of times I longed to be an only child, but now, as the years have passed, the joy of having a sister has far outweighed any frustration. And as I have learned to share with her, she has taught me a few lessons too – like: it is much easier to laugh when you have someone to laugh with, the nights aren't nearly as dark when someone is sharing your room, and being an only child couldn't be nearly as fun as having another child with whom I can play, giggle, and share.

Share
by Jessie Baldwin

While an adult created this layout, it illustrates two things of relevance to children. The journaling doesn't have to go on the front—it can go on the back as seen here. Putting it on the back keeps the focus on the photo. Also, children can journal about lessons they've learned by being an only child or by being a sibling. What are the pros and cons?

SUPPLIES: Patterned paper by Wordsworth and 7 Gypsies (definitions). Cardstock by Bazzil. Together font is CK Bella; journaling font is Garamond. Circle clip is from Jest Charming Embellishments. Gold floss is from DMD and page pebble is from Making Memories.

Love begins at home, and it is not how much we do...but how much love we put in that action.
—Mother Theresa

When peoples care for you and cry for you, they can straighten out your soul.
—Langston Hughes

Prompts to trigger journaling

- ❏ What do you like best about your mom? What is your mother's best trait? What makes her different from your friends' moms?

- ❏ What traits of your mother's do you see in yourself?

- ❏ What do you like best about your dad? What is your father's best trait? What makes him different from your friends' dads?

- ❏ What traits of your father's do you see in yourself?

- ❏ Write a want ad that describes your father.

- ❏ Write a want ad that describes your mother.

- ❏ Complete this statement: I am proud of my mom/dad for...

- ❏ I am glad my parents taught me...

- ❏ What do you like about being a son or daughter in your family? What do you like best about each member of your family?

- ❏ Were you first-born, middle child, the baby or somewhere in between? Do you like your place in the family? What are the pros and cons?

- ❏ Do you have brothers and/or sisters? Do you play well together or fight a lot? How do you get along?

- ❏ What do you like best about being a brother or sister? What do you like least?

- ❏ Do you wish you had more brothers or sisters? Why?

- ❏ Draw a picture of your family.

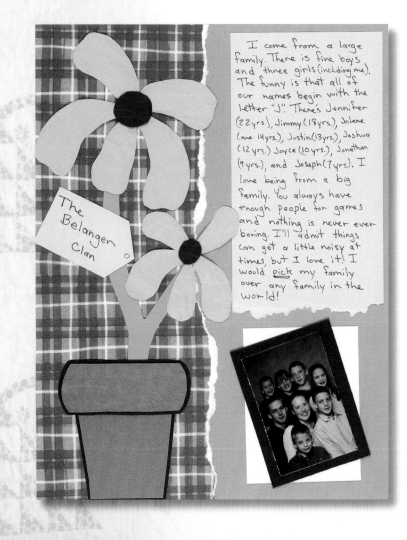

I come from a large family. There is five boys and three girls (including me). The funny is that all of our names begin with the letter "J". There's Jennifer (22 yrs.), Jimmy (18 yrs.), Jolene (me 14 yrs.), Justin (13 yrs.), Joshua (12 yrs.) Joyce (10 yrs.), Jonathan (9 yrs.), and Joseph (7 yrs.). I love being from a big family. You always have enough people for games and nothing is never ever boring. I'll admit things can get a little noisy at times, but I love it! I would pick my family over any family in the world!

The Belanger Clan

The Belanger Clan
by Jolene Belanger, age 14

Jolene's journaling includes all of the details to describe her family—names, ages and what she likes best (despite the noise level generated by eight kids in one family!). Note that she combined a small picture with a large paper-piecing to give a sense of balance to the layout.

SUPPLIES: Patterned paper is by Mustard Moon; cardstock is by Serendipity. Lettering and flower paper-piecing are both by Jolene.

- Do you go on family vacations? What's been your favorite vacation? What did you do? How did you get there? Who went with you on the trip? Did you get to help with the planning? Did anything funny or memorable ever happen?

- Make a list of "Fun Things We Do Together." This could be movies, sporting events, theatre productions, cultural events, etc. What do you like to do best? What fun things do you do together that are free?

- Do your parents read to you? What are your favorite books at story time?

- Do you think you will be a good parent? What do you want for your children?

- Does your mom or dad make any recipes that you will want to pass on to your children? Where did the recipes come from?

- Describe the first home you lived in. Was it an apartment, a house in the city, a rural farmhouse? Include addresses if you can remember them.

- Draw a floor plan of your home and label the rooms.

- Who lives with you? Any extended family? Do you share a bedroom with anyone? What do you like and dislike about that?

*There's no vocabulary
For love within a family,
love that's lived in
But not looked at, love
within the light of which
All else is seen, the love
within which
All other love finds speech.
This love is silent.*

—T.S. Eliot

*A family in harmony will
prosper in everything.*
—Chinese Proverb

*One rich family is envied
by a thousand others.*
—Chinese Proverb

all night talks about really cute boys:)

"Rock Around the Clock" playing restaurant for hours

Cousins BY CHANCE friends BY CHOICE

stealing eachothers haircuts (grandma did that)

sleepovers at grandmas

sleeping with the nightlight on

kelsie and kassidy

playing pretend in your bunk-bed/play kitchen

JUNE 02

Cousins by Chance, Friends by Choice
by Kassidy Christensen, age 15

Note how Kassidy included "proof" of how she and her cousin are friends. The little strips of vellum provide a glimpse into the fun they've had together.

SUPPLIES: Patterned paper is by Made to Match. Stickers are by Provo Craft and My Mind's Eye. Journaling font is CK Constitution. Eyelets and vellum were also used.

If the family were a container, it would be a nest, an enduring nest, loosely woven, expansive, and open. If the family were a fruit, it would be an orange, a circle of sections, held together but separable—each segment distinct. If the family were a boat, it would be a canoe that makes no progress unless everyone paddles.

　　　　—Letty Cottin Pogrebin

Family jokes, though rightly cursed by strangers, are the bond that keeps most families alive.

　　　　—Stella Benson

In truth a family is what you make it. It is made strong, not by number of heads counted at the dinner table, but by the rituals you help family members create, by the memories you share, by the commitment of time, caring, and love you show to one another, and by the hopes for the future you have as individuals and as a unit.

　　　　—Marge Kennedy

A big family must be fun. I imagine it makes you feel you belong to something.

　　　　—Barré Lyndon and Byron Haskins

❏ Where do your grandparents live? What was their home like? Did it have a certain 'smell' or 'look' or 'feel'?

❏ What makes a family strong? How is your family strong? Why are families important?

❏ Do you have any family chores or duties?

❏ Does your family have any pets? Do a layout about your family pet(s). What kind of animal is it? When did you get your pet? What funny things does your pet do? What kind of pet would you like to have? Draw a picture of your pet.

❏ What is your family's cultural heritage? Do you practice any cultural traditions? Research customs, stories, traditions, foods and clothing on the Internet.

❏ Construct a family tree. Go back two generations to include yourself, your parents, your grandparents and your great-grandparents.

❏ Tell about any ancestors that you know about. Include names and dates, etc. for historical purposes and any stories about them.

❏ What are your "genetic ingredients"? Who do you look like— your mom or your dad? A combination of both? Who did you get your nose from? The color of your eyes? Your left-handedness?

❏ What are your family's "house rules"?

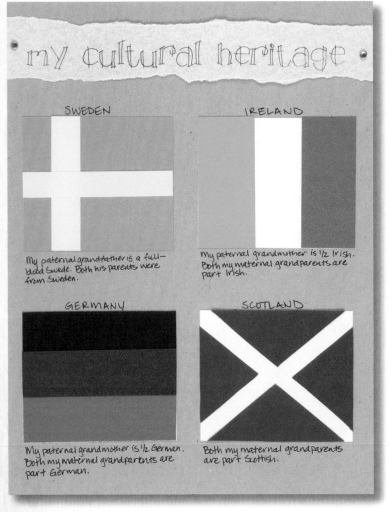

My Cultural Heritage
by Angie Pedersen

This layout can come together pretty quickly once you have your genealogical information on countries of origin. You can find flags at education.yahoo.com/reference/factbook/. Using the pictures found there, I recreated the flags using cardstock scraps. I noted which relative came from which country in the caption under each flag. This is a neat way to visually represent all of the pieces that contribute to one's cultural heritage.

SUPPLIES: Title font is 2Ps Rustic that is traced onto vellum. Brads are by Boxer Scrapbooks.

- ❑ What are some things your parents always say?
- ❑ Describe a typical Saturday in your family.
- ❑ How do you show your family you love them? How do they show you they love you?
- ❑ What's the funniest thing that's ever happened in your family? Draw a comic strip to tell the story.
- ❑ Create a Family Timeline. Include major moves, births, starting school, favorite vacations and any other important historical dates in your family.
- ❑ If you were a mouse in your house, what might you see your family doing?

- ❑ Do you have any family heirlooms? Describe them and how you came to acquire them.
- ❑ What are some holiday traditions in your family? How do you celebrate festive times?
- ❑ Describe your mother's wedding dress. What do you know about her wedding?
- ❑ Describe your yard. Do you help with the yard work? What are your favorite backyard memories? Draw a diagram if you can.
- ❑ Do you and either parent or provider share an interest in any hobbies or activities? Do you participate in any special activities together?
- ❑ Do you still see or do you remember any of your grandparents?

www.

Coloring page for the Chinese character for "family":
www.childbook.com/images/coloring/family.jpg

Microsoft Design Gallery Clipart (search "family"):
dgl.microsoft.com/

Plan fun things to do with your family:
familyfun.go.com/

The Legacy Project: activities to do with family and grandparents:
www.tcpnow.com/legacy/legacyproject.html

Find pictures of different country's flags for a Cultural Heritage layout:
education.yahoo.com/reference/factbook/flags/a.html

Sample lesson plan for an introduction to genealogy and family trees:
tepserver.ucsd.edu/~eaguilar/Family%20Tree/WebQuest

Download and print off general genealogy forms, including a family tree template:
www.familytreemagazine.com/forms/download.html

Lesson plan idea for creating a Personal Dictionary:
www.twc.org/forums/writers_on_teaching/fwir_labrown.html

chi gong

I love my Daddy. I like doing chi gong with Daddy. We do nibbles on our face, and pound on our legs and arms, that's part of chi gong. We stretch backwards and upwards, we wiggle our heads, and we try not to fall with our feet up. We do chi gong because it's lots of exercise, and that's how I like it.

Chi Gong *by Adira Tova Balbac, age 2*

Adira was not yet three years old when she did this layout. Her mom had created a larger layout with more pictures of her doing Chi Gong with her father and she asked for these two pictures for her own book. Adira dictated the journaling, made the color and layout decisions and adhered the photos onto the pages. Adira's mom liked Adira's journaling better than the journaling that she had written on the same topic.

SUPPLIES: Font is Bradley Hand.

Any greats? What are their names? Did you have a close relationship with any of your grandparents? Describe any memories that you have. Draw a picture of your favorite thing to do with Grandma or Grandpa.

❑ How do you cure hiccups in your home? Any other funny remedies that your family uses?

❑ Create a family dictionary. What are some things your family says that you don't think other families say?

Photos to find or request

❑ A picture of the whole family
❑ Pictures of ancestors

❑ A picture of your child, from head to toe (for "Genetic Ingredients")
❑ A picture of each set of grandparents
❑ A picture of a holiday celebration
❑ Picture(s) of past home(s)

Pictures to take

❑ A picture of your child's room
❑ A picture of your child's current home
❑ Pictures of family heirlooms
❑ Pictures of grandparents
❑ Pictures of pet(s)
❑ A picture of a favorite family meal

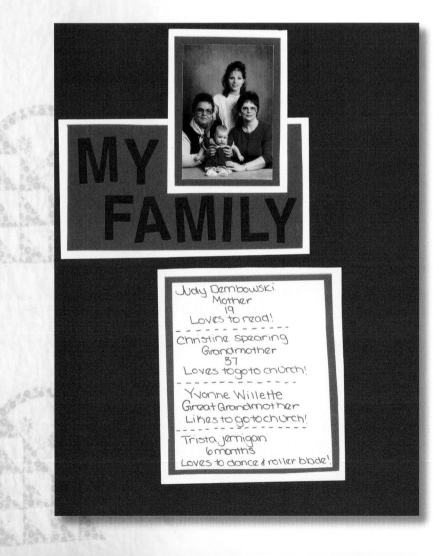

My Family
by Trista Jernigan, age 14

Trista included great details in her journaling—name, relationship, age and one personal detail. This layout quickly captures the essence of four generations!

SUPPLIES: Cardstock by Serendipity. Hand lettering by Trista.

3: My School

Children spend approximately 35 hours a week in school. This is practically a full-time job for them; it deserves to be scrapped! All these hours add up to days, months, and ultimately, years—that's a lot of memories!

Why is this theme important?

School introduces children to different ways of thinking, ways of approaching and solving problems, and new ideas in general. It also broadens their social life to a circle larger than their immediate family.

By "school" I mean kindergarten through senior year, though your child may want to separate elementary, middle and high school years into individual sections. The prompts offered below could be asked and re-asked through the years and can apply to any year in school.

For those times when you don't have pictures of school adventures, children can still preserve those memories. For the first day of school, I send my son to school with a disposable camera—he gets to record his perspective on the beginning of a new year. I get the benefit of a view of his life that I miss since I'm not with him.

I also send a disposable camera for special field trips and Field Day. If the camera gets left behind (or sat

In this section we'll look at time spent at school. School may come in several different forms. For our purposes, school is wherever your child spends the majority of his or her time learning.

Mr. Teddy Bear
by Kennedy Wools, age 8

Kennedy used letter stickers for her journaling that described one of her homework assignments from school. She also drew her own bear on cardstock and cut it out to include in the layout. Children's art makes great, one-of-a-kind embellishments.

SUPPLIES: Large letter stickers are by Creative Memories; mini letter stickers are by Making Memories.

I had to take care. Of our
classbear KENNE
DYBIG BEAR

No entertainment is as cheap as reading, nor any pleasure so lasting.

—Lady Mary Wortley Montagu

The man who can make hard things easy is the educator.

—Ralph Waldo Emerson

It is the supreme art of the teacher to awaken joy in creative expression and knowledge.

—Albert Einstein

on), I'm not out much. But if the camera does make it home, more stories can be told.

Children don't seem to have hang-ups creating layouts with just journaling and stickers, so let them be creative. Ask them what they remember most about a certain person, activity or subject. Find some stickers or a paper-piecing to illustrate it.

You can also ask your child what particular memories he or she wants to document and send a disposable camera with them to school to specifically take pictures of related things.

By encouraging your child to take photos of things that are important to him or her, you are reinforcing that their thoughts and memories are worth documenting. What a confidence builder! You're also reinforcing that school is an important part of life and that school is a priority in your family.

In my children's scrapbooks...

James created layouts on his favorite subject in school, on being accepted into the district gifted program and the friends he plays with at recess. Joanne made a layout on bringing home the class pet for the weekend. She also plans to create layouts on three things she likes about kindergarten and her favorite bus driver.

Creative Writing
by Breanne Crawford, age 18

Torn strips on the border are used to list things that happened and inside jokes from Breanne's creative writing class. Journaling for similar class layouts could also include a list of friends in the class, fun learning activities or field trips.

SUPPLIES: Plaid paper is by Northern Spy. Border paper is from Renae Lindgren for Creative Imaginations.

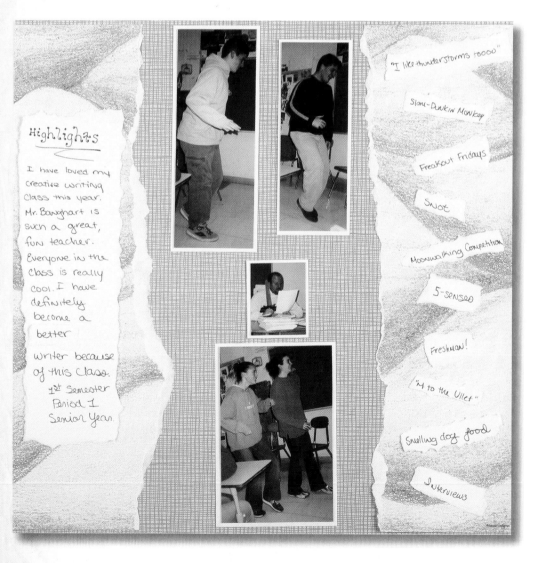

Prompts to trigger journaling

- What were/are your favorite subjects in school? Your least favorite?

- Describe the history of your school. When was it built? What its mascot? How many students attend the school? Name three things you like best about your school. Interview three friends about what they like best about your school.

- Describe a typical day at elementary/middle/high school/ homeschool.

- What did/do you do at recess? Who did/do you play with?

- Do you or did you participate in any extracurricular clubs or activities like band, choir or student newspaper? Describe the group(s), the meetings and the members.

- Describe memorable field trips.

- Interview your principal and include three facts you didn't know on a layout.

- If you are homeschooled, do a layout that includes a typical daily schedule. Where do school and homelife meet? Where is your classroom? What are the pros and cons of homeschooling for you?

- Interview your teacher. Why did he or she decide to become a teacher? Does your teacher enjoy the job?

A master can tell you what he expects of you.
A teacher, though, awakens your own expectations.
—Patricia Neal

Education is not filling a bucket, but lighting a fire.
—William Yeats

The mediocre teacher tells. The good teacher explains. The superior teacher demonstrates. The great teacher inspires.
—William Arthur Ward

Mon Voyage Français
by Amanda Goodwin, age 16

Amanda's layout illustrates the fun she has participating in French Club at school. Note her attention to design detail—journaling on vellum that is eyeletted over patterned paper, key words highlighted in red chalk, focal-point photo torn and chalked and even a paper-pieced French flag! All of these elements help the layout stand out.

SUPPLIES: Patterned paper is by Printworks. Buttons are by Making Memories. Chalk is by Craf-T Products. Eyelets are by Doodlebug Design. Fonts are 2Peas Tuxedo and 2Peas Dainty.

❑ Have you ever run for Student Council? What position? How did the election turn out?

❑ Where do you most often do homework and study? Did you study with others, or alone? Do you make good grades?

❑ What are you studying this year? Do you enjoy it? What do you like best?

❑ What's your favorite school lunch? Who do you sit with at lunch?

❑ What is your favorite special class: music, art or gym? Why? What's your favorite activity in that class?

❑ Who is your favorite teacher? What subject does he or she teach? Why is he or she a good teacher. What have you learned from him or her? Make a list of things you've learned from this teacher. Try using bulleted journaling or a top 10 list.

❑ What's in your backpack? Make a list of everything you usually keep in your backpack and tell why each thing is in there.

❑ What's your favorite thing to do after school?

❑ Create a pocket page for school awards, certificates and report cards.

❑ What has been the most fun activity at school so far?

❑ Draw a map of your school. What rooms do you visit most often? Which teacher is in which room?

Brain Strain
by Linda Abrams, journaling by Elayna Fremes, age 14

This layout documents Elayna's first high school exams. Linda did the layout and Elayna did the journaling. Future generations will be able to read that while Elayna may have struggled with the test preparations, her hard work was rewarded in the end.

SUPPLIES: Patterned paper and stickers are by Making Memories. Frame is by Cock-a-Doodle Designs.

Photos to find or request

- ❑ School pictures
- ❑ Field trip activities
- ❑ Extracurricular events
- ❑ Homework sessions
- ❑ Report cards
- ❑ Awards
- ❑ Class pictures

Pictures to take

- ❑ The school and mascot
- ❑ Teachers
- ❑ School friends
- ❑ The cafeteria
- ❑ Special classrooms (like gym, music or art)
- ❑ Textbooks spread out
- ❑ Backpack filled with school stuff
- ❑ Desk or locker at school

Whenever you are asked if you can do a job, tell 'em, 'Certainly I can!' Then get busy and find out how to do it.
—Theodore Roosevelt

Curiosity is the wick in the candle of learning.
—William A. Ward

Education is learning what you didn't even know you didn't know.
—Daniel Boorstin

Awards Ceremony
by Mindy Dunlap, age 14

This layout gives an idea of how to document awards received at school. Kids can include the actual award certificate and a photo of them holding or receiving the award.

SUPPLIES: Patterned paper, stickers, die cuts and punches are from Creative Memories. Journaling was hand lettered with a silver pen.

www.

Research your school's history and mascot at the school website! Ask your librarian if you don't know the URL.

Lesson plan on creating a school e-newspaper: commtechlab.msu.edu/ sites/letsnet/noframes/ Subjects/la/b6u3.html

Rules and directions for a variety of games to play during recess: www.gameskidsplay.net

Make a big welcome book to make new students feel welcome in your classroom: www.eduplace.com/ activity/bigbk.html

Create a school time capsule: www.eduplace.com/ activity/mytime.html

Plan a playground pickup to help your school: pbskids.org/zoom/action/ way08.html

Create and play a game of school trivia: www.teachers.net/lessons/ posts//595.html

School-themed fonts: www.fortunecity.com/ skyscraper/dos/1232/ page06.html

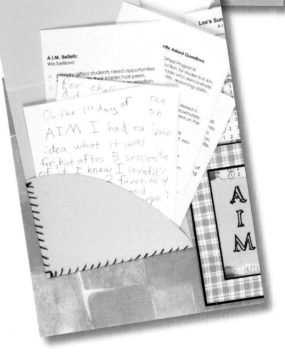

A.I.M. High!
by Angie Pedersen,
journaling by James Pedersen, age 9

Pockets are a great way to "corral" all of the memorabilia that comes home from school. Here, I borrowed an idea from Shari Rademacher and used a pre-made die cut frame for the big pocket that holds the progress report. I still had more to include on the layout, so I made another pocket underneath the photo by folding a long strip of cardstock in half to make a book. Then, I stitched the scrap of cardstock onto the back piece of the book to make a pocket.

Supplies: Patterned paper by Karen Foster. Die cut frame by My Mind's Eye. Fonts are New Romantics ("A.I.M. High!"), Doodle ("A.I.M." on pocket); 2Ps Evergreen ("chieve", "nspire", and "otivate" on pocket); and Century Gothic (journaling in pocket under photo).

4: My Friends

My son describes a friend as "Someone you can trust, do fun things with and talk to." Sounds pretty accurate to me.

On pages about friendship, children can highlight their take on what friendship means. For some kids, this may mean creating pages about places they go and things they do together. For other kids, this may mean layouts more like tributes—how they met, what they admire about them and why they get along well.

Your job here is to suggest a combination of both. For those kids who lean toward the basics—"We went to the zoo and had fun," you can suggest that they dig a little deeper for journaling details.

Here are some basic questions with which you can guide the child's journaling:

❏ How and when did you meet this friend?

❏ What made you want to meet them?

❏ What did you do together (in these photos)?

❏ What do you like best about this friend?

❏ What makes you and your friend laugh together?

In this section, children can explore not only what it means to be a friend, but also they can be a friend to others.

Best Friends Pocket Page
by Kelcie Thomas, age 12

Kelcie created this pocket page to hold notes from friends. The pocket could also hold pictures of her with her friends.

Supplies: Patterned paper is by Scrap in a Snap. Page topper is by Beary Patch. Hand lettering is by Kelcie Thomas.

Never shall I forget the time I spent with you. Please continue to be my friend, as you will always find me yours.
    —Ludwig van Beethoven

Friendship is a union of spirits, a marriage of hearts, and bond there of virtue.
    —Samuel Johnson

❑ What have you learned from your friends?

❑ What rituals do you have together? What do you do every time you get together?

❑ How do you know this person is your friend—what actions or behaviors make them stand out as a friend?

Why is this theme important?

This role is important because friends play an integral role in a child's development. Many impressions your child draws about himself are inferred from friends.

Highlighting the positive points of a friendship allows your child to realize how important friendship is, as well as reinforcing the basic definition of friendship. When

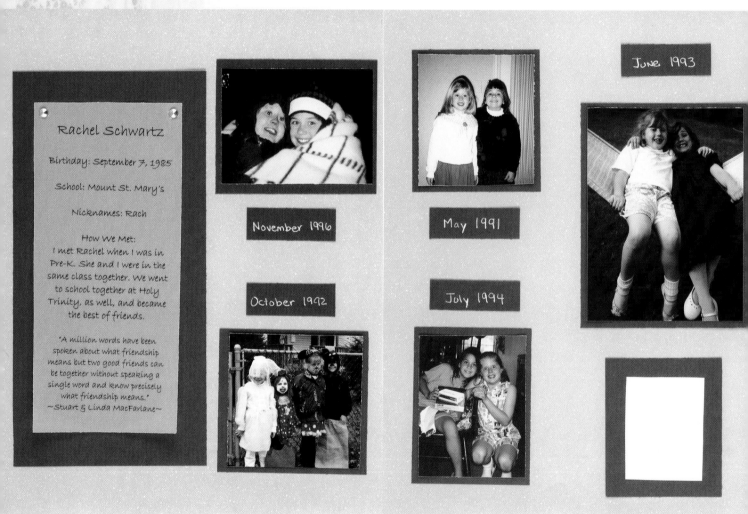

Rachel Schwartz
by Breanne Crawford, age 18

Breanne uses great details—name, birthday, current school, nickname and how they met—to preserve her memories of her friend. And how cool that she has photos spanning five years of friendship! You could adapt this idea to create a "Through the Years" layout on one of your child's long-term friendships. Note how Breanne left a spot for a current photo.

SUPPLIES: Patterned paper is by Keeping Memories Alive. Title and journaling font is Bradley Hand.

your child sits down to think about what friendship has brought into his or her life, he or she might be more likely to work at strengthening current friendships, as well as personally striving to be a better friend.

When your child takes time out to think about priorities (i.e. spending time with good friends) and how he or she is already acting on those priorities, it reinforces to your child all the good things experienced on a daily basis. That's cause for celebration (as well as a number of scrapbook pages).

In my children's scrapbooks...

My son is planning to do pages on friends he has met through various venues—school friends, friends from the lake, friends from karate and friends from scouts. He plans to journal about the different things they do together and funny memories he has. (Humor plays big with this kid!)

My daughter wants to do a page about friends from each of her former preschools now that she has moved on to kindergarten. It is important to her to remember them since she won't see them every day.

Friendship is sharing openly, laughing often, trusting always and caring deeply.
—Unknown

We'll be best friends until forever, wait and see.
—Winnie the Pooh

A friend is someone you can do nothing with and enjoy it.
—Unknown

*To me, fair friend, you never can be old
For as you were when first your eye I eyed,
Such seems your beauty still.*
—William Shakespeare

Lucky Me
by Breanne Crawford, age 18

With this layout, Breanne pays homage to her two closest friends as well as to her own blessings. Breanne's journaling reveals how she considers her friends blessings in her life and what she appreciates most about them. Consider doing a layout on how your child's friends make him or her feel lucky or blessed.

SUPPLIES: Title stickers are by Me & My Big Ideas. Die cuts are by O'Scrap Accents.

You and I are what friend-ship is all about.

— Paula Finn

No matter where life may take us, some friendships are forever.

—Flavia

I count myself in nothing else so happy as in a soul remem-bering my good friends.

—William Shakespeare

Prompts to trigger journaling

❑ Where and how did you meet?

❑ What do you do (or did you do) with your friends?

❑ What do you like or admire about them?

❑ How are you alike and different?

❑ What have you learned from your friends?

❑ What do you talk about?

❑ Include "testimonials" written by friends

  o Their favorite things about you

  o First and current impressions of you

  o What have they learned from you?

  o What do they admire about you?

❑ What makes a good friend? How are *you* a good friend?

❑ Write a letter to your best friend. Thank this person for being your friend.

❑ What's the funniest thing that's ever happened with your friend(s)?

❑ How has your friend(s) helped you through a hard time?

❑ What do you miss most about friends you no longer see?

Wonderland by *Valeria Chiappetta, age 18*

Note how Valeria used bright colored squares of cardstock to mat her photos and the stickers. The stickers add a lot more to the layout when they are part of the grid design. This is an easy layout for kids to recreate and use the stickers they love so much. It is also a great design for using random photos of friends.

SUPPLIES: Stickers are by Me & My Big Ideas. Hand lettering is by Valeria.

Photos to find or request

- ❑ Photos of you with each of your close friends
- ❑ Photos of your friend's house
- ❑ Photos of places you frequent (pool, park, restaurant, store, etc.)
- ❑ Photos of school(s) you have attended together
- ❑ Photos of trips you've taken together
- ❑ Silly photos taken at slumber parties, photo booths, or makeovers.

Pictures to take

- ❑ Pocket page for notes from friends
- ❑ Ticket stubs for concerts you attended with your friends
- ❑ Brochures for places to which you traveled, or sites you toured
- ❑ Menu from restaurants you frequent
- ❑ Recipe for your favorite "pig-out" food

"We'll be friends forever, won't we, Pooh?" asked Piglet.
"Even longer," Pooh answered.

—Winnie the Pooh

A friend is someone who knows who you are, understands where you've been, accepts who you have become and still invites you to grow.

—Unknown

Paige
Brower

Paige is my friend, but she is moving to Oregon. She is four years old. We do jobs together like the toothpick job. We play outside together. We dig in the sandbox and the tanbark. We go up the steps, then we go down the slide, then we do it again. I'm going to miss her.   *Dec 2002*

Paige Brower *by Adira Tova Balzac*

This is the first layout Adira did at age two years 10 months. Her Montessori school teacher slipped the photo in her cubby and her mom knew that this would be a good time to get Adira started on scrapping. She chose the colors and scissors patterns and dictated the journaling. Her mom showed her different layout options and read the journaling back to her until Adira said that she had it right. Adira glued the topper and put the photo down with splits.

Supplies: Decorative scissors by Fiskars.

Friends bring sunshine and color into our lives, allowing us to see the quiet beauty of everyday things.

—Unknown

Remember, the greatest gift is not found in a store nor under a tree, but in the hearts of true friends.

—Cindy Lew

Life's truest happiness is found in friendships we make along the way.

—Unknown

A friend is someone who sees through you and still enjoys the view.

—Wilma Askinas

Don't be dismayed at good-byes. A farewell is necessary before you can meet again. And meeting again, after moments or lifetimes, is certain for those who are friends.

—Richard Bach

Listening is a magnetic and strange thing, a creative force. The friends who listen to us are the ones we move toward. When we are listened to, it creates us, makes us unfold and expand.

—Karl Menninger

No love, no friendship can cross the path of our destiny without leaving some mark on it forever.

—Francois Mauriac

I met Laurel in junior high through Kirsten. Laurel was later in ballet classes with us, and I had theater classes with her in high school. She played my future Mother In Law in "You Can't Take It With You". Last time I saw her was in 1999 at our 10-year reunion.

SS **OF** **1989**

TRISTA ETZIG   MIKE EAGAN   MIKKA GEE   MEG JOHNSON

BROOKE SHADEL   STACEY NEFF   STEVE THOMPSON   KATY STEINBACHER

Friends—Class of 1989 *by Jessica Shawl*

What a great way to showcase all of those senior pictures. In this layout, each photo mat opens up to reveal the message written on the back of the photo and Jessica's journaling.

SUPPLIES: Stickers are by Mrs. Grossman's. Title font is YrBkMess (www.coolarchive.com); journaling font is Bookworm.

WWW.

How is your friendship like a heroic journey?: serv1.ncte.org/teach/ Dundore12297.shtml

Friendship quotes: www.famous-quotes-and-quotations.com/friendship-quotes.html

Search for friendship poetry at dMarie.com: dmarie.com/asp/poems.asp ?action=queryform

Friendship poems and quotes: www.friendship-poems.com/index.html

Friendship theme unit for the classroom: www.kinderkorner.com/ friends.html

Make a friendship bracelet (and include it on a page): www.makingfriends.com/ friendship.htm

Make a paper doll that looks like your friend: www.makingfriends.com/ f_Friends.htm

5: MY TEAMS & GROUPS

This section looks at preserving the memories your child creates as a member of a group. That group could be scouts, a sports team or an extra-curricular club like chess, debate, drama or 4-H.

When children join a group or club, it's often because their friends are members or the activity appeals to them. But being part of a group is much more than just a social outlet. Through group activities, children learn about cooperation, teamwork, good sportsmanship, leadership, perseverance and loyalty. They learn what it means to contribute to a larger whole.

Consider what kinds of groups your child joins, what he does with those groups, the level of his participation and how being a member of a group has affected his life.

Many kids create layouts with multiple photos of soccer practices and games, but with very little meaningful journaling. The journaling is what will help your child look back later and remember what meant the most to him about these activities.

You can encourage your children to include journaling about what being a team member means, how each member depends on the other members of the group and what talents and gifts each child contributes to a group. Expressing these thoughts through journaling may also reinforce how much the group means to your child, and how the group will help in challenging

Friends

by Jolene Belanger, age 14

Participating in group activities often gives a person a sense of belonging. In this layout, Jolene describes just that. To illustrate this sense of identity, Jolene tells about a specific instance when her team definitely "stood out in the crowd" by dressing like fairies! What examples can you think of when one of your child's groups or teams did something silly to get noticed?

SUPPLIES: Cardstock by Serendipity. Hand lettering is by Jolene.

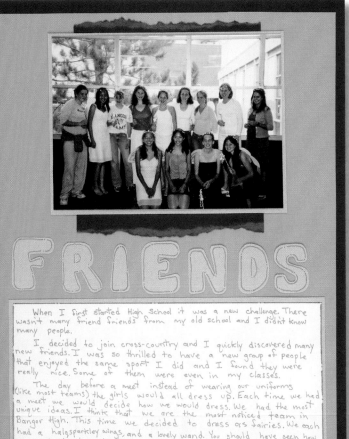

times when he or she may want to quit. Preserving those countless photos of games, concerts, meetings and so on is great, but you can ask the leading questions that will help document the memories more fully.

Why is this theme important?

So much of children's free time is spent in organized group activities, whether scouts, sports, or whatever. Not only is the time spent considerable, but children also learn a number of life lessons in group activities.

They practice social skills and strive to improve motor and cognitive skills. Organized group activities provide a different dynamic than that found in school—generally clubs or teams represent a choice, a voluntary decision to join. This says a lot about your child's personal interests. This deserves to be scrapped so that the full memory is preserved.

In my children's scrapbooks...

My son did pages on what he likes best about Cub Scouts. He also made a page on how he doesn't always like group violin lessons but enjoys being able to play the violin. My daughter plans to do layouts on gymnastic classes and Daisy Scouts. (She's very excited about joining when she is in kindergarten, and is already picking out daisy stickers for her stash!).

When you're part of a team, you stand up for your teammates. Your loyalty is to them. You protect them through good and bad, because they'd do the same for you.

—Yogi Berra

The greater the loyalty of a group toward the group, the greater is the motivation among the members to achieve the goals of the group, and the greater the probability that the group will achieve its goals.

—Rensis Likert

Talent wins games, but teamwork and intelligence win championships.

—Michael Jordan

...there are extraordinary men and women and extraordinary moments when history leaps forward on the backs of these individuals, that what can be imagined can be achieved, that you must dare to dream, but that there's no substitute for perseverance and hard work and teamwork because no one gets there alone.

—Dana Scully, "X-Files"

Twinkle Toes *by Kennedy Wools, age 18*
This layout pictures Kennedy "in action" at dance class. Action or candid shots really help portray the essence of the group. Kennedy's journaling promotes another key point—she describes what she likes best about her classes—she has lots of "frens". Other layouts about group physical activities could include journaling about the hardest moves or skills to learn and how long it took to learn them.

SUPPLIES: Butterfly sticker by Frances Meyer; other stickers by Stickabilities.

I once thought I could protect the world by myself, but I was wrong. Working together, we saved the planet and I believe that if we stayed together as a team, we could be a force that could truly work for the ideals of peace and justice.

    —Superman

There are few, if any, jobs in which ability alone is sufficient. Needed, also, are loyalty, sincerity, enthusiasm and team play.

   —William B. Given, Jr.

A single arrow is easily broken, but not ten in a bundle.

   —Japanese proverb

It is amazing how much people can get done if they do not worry about who gets the credit.

   —Sandra Swinney

More Than a Team

by Kassidy Christensen, age 15

Kassidy used letter stamps to include some of the private jokes she's enjoyed as part of this team. She also included a combination of formal group and candid photos.

SUPPLIES: Patterned paper is by All My Memories. Stickers are by David Walker, Colorbok.

Prompts to trigger journaling

❑ What groups have you joined? Consider groups based in:
- o Spiritual organization
- o The Internet
- o Local hobby groups
- o Local advocacy groups
- o Physical fitness/sports
- o School
- o Neighborhood
- o Support groups
- o Scouts
- o 4-H or FFA

❑ How long have you been a member? How often and where do you meet?

❑ What do you do at meetings? What was the most fun activity?

❑ Do you make anything with the group? Do a page on several completed projects.

❑ Do you wear a uniform? What badges and patches have you earned?

❑ What awards have you earned in the group? How long did it take you to earn it?

❑ Tell about exciting or funny experiences in religious groups, scouting, sports teams, etc.

❑ Who are your leaders? What are some things they always say? What do they say about teamwork, hard work and practice?

❑ Who are your friends?

❑ What do you like best about the group?

midnight chats pep talks team chants **MORE than a TEAM** warm up games inside jokes hot guys

- ❑ Where have you gone with the groups you have joined?
- ❑ Did you go camping with any group? Tell about your experiences.
- ❑ How do you volunteer to help the group? What leadership positions have you held? What are or were your job duties?
- ❑ What have you learned as a result of participating in a group? Songs? Skills? Techniques? Life lessons?

Photos to find or request

- ❑ Group photos for each group or association
- ❑ Photo of your child at a group activity

- ❑ Photo of a meeting
- ❑ Photo or scan of the group mascot or logo
- ❑ Photo of your child holding an award from the group

Pictures to take

- ❑ Photo of close friends from the group
- ❑ Photo of the place where the group meets
- ❑ Photo of the group uniform
- ❑ Samples from group demo's of craft techniques
- ❑ Photos from field trips the group takes

What I do you cannot do; but what you do, I cannot do. The needs are great, and none of us, including me, ever do great things. But we can all do small things, with great love, and together we can do something wonderful.
—Mother Teresa

A boat doesn't go forward if each one is rowing their own way.
—Swahili proverb

Great discoveries and improvements invariably involve the cooperation of many minds.
—Alexander Graham Bell

My Uniform
by Sharon Mehl

This is a great testament to all the work it takes that goes into being a scout. Sharon photographed her son's uniform and included close-up shots of specific patches. She takes photos yearly to show her son's progress. Then, she documents what it took to earn each award.

Kids could do similar layouts documenting a specific project they worked on and how long it took to complete the project or award. This reminds children that success takes hard work. It also reminds them of the pride of accomplishment.

SUPPLIES: Patterned paper is by Scrap-Ease. Die cut is by Per-snippity. Stencil is by EZ2Cut. Cub Scout Stick Kid is by Stamping Station.

WWW.

Boy Scouting home page:
www.scouting.org/
index.html

Girl Scouting home page:
www.girlscouts.org/

National 4H Council:
www.fourhcouncil.edu/

CDC website on physical
fitness for kids:
www.bam.gov/index.htm

Organize a kids help
group in your neighbor-
hood:
www.nick.com/all_nick/
specials/bighelp/bh_
water.jhtml

Pack an emergency activ-
ity kit so your group will
always have something
to do:
www.scoutbase.org.uk/
activity/cubs/whatno/
basickit.htm

Plan all sorts of neat activities for your group:
www.macscouter.com/

**Tallmadge Major
All-Stars**
by Amanda Goodwin, age 16

Amanda created this lay-
out for her sister using fun
group photos along with
a program from an event
signed by all of the players.

This layout concept could
be used for all different
kinds of groups—you can
substitute a program cover
with a piece of cardstock
and have everyone in the
group sign it and include
it on a layout with a group
photo. Including people's
signatures and handwrit-
ing lets you preserve a little
piece of their personalities
in your scrapbooks.

*Supplies: Patterned paper is by
Kangaroo & Joey. Stickers are
by SEI.*

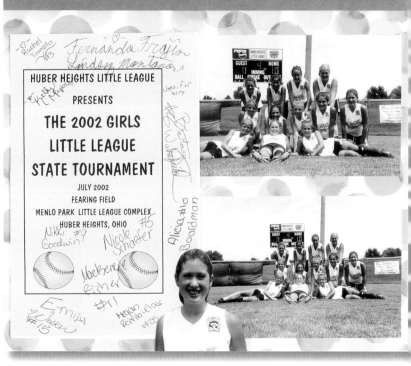

Sports Camp
*by Linda Abrams, journaling
by Josh Fremes, age 9*

Linda created this layout
and Josh, her nine-year-old
son, wrote the journaling.
Linda thinks that it is important to have the journaling
written by kids, in their
own handwriting, and from
their perspective. Linda put
the vellum envelope on the
outside of the page protec-
tor so the journaling is ac-
cessible.

*Supplies: Patterned paper is by
Hot Off the Press. Frame is by
Cock-a-Doodle Designs. Page
topper is computer generated.*

6: MY CHARACTER

If you watch the TV series "Star Trek" for any length of time, you will probably hear a crew member refer to "hull integrity". The integrity of the hull is its status, how strong it is. Can the hull be depended on to last through the current battle? Will it continue to hold everything together in a cohesive whole?

One's personal integrity can be viewed the same way. Your integrity is what sees you through life's challenges. If we encourage children to document how they are living a life of integrity, they will start to recognize their own achievements in these areas. They can also pinpoint areas they wish to develop.

As adults, we can provide opportunities for character education for our children, so they are more likely to meet this ideal. When we do, we set the stage for future development on your child's terms. We can further this development by encouraging children to scrap it.

The key here is to guide children to dig deeper in their journaling, to focus on key traits and honor their place in their lives. One way we can do this may be saying, "Wow! That guy must have been really brave! What do you think he was thinking

This section focuses on your children's sense of right and wrong, "fair play" and how they can act around others.

Courage
by Angie Pedersen

To create the background paper with Chinese characters, I chose the characters I wanted to use (courage, strength, hope and will). Then, I typed those characters into rows using the SBChinese dingbat font. I printed it out and used it as an accent. The journaling points out three instances when my son exhibited courage.

Supplies: Patterned paper is by Wordsworth. Fonts are SBChinese (www.ontariolive.com/jole-fonts), Century Gothic, John Doe and A&S Harlequin.

3 times I've shown COURAGE

- Performing a violin solo & jokes at the All-School Talent Show
- Campaigning for 4th Grade Student Council
- Ignoring bullies on the bus

勇
courage

Courage \Cour'age\, n. That quality of mind which enables one to encounter danger and difficulties with firmness, or without fear, or fainting of heart; valor; boldness; resolution.

Do not attempt to do a thing unless you are sure of yourself; but do not relinquish it because someone else is not sure of you.

—Stewart White

Be happy with what you have and you will have plenty to be happy about.

—Irish Proverb

A mistake is not something to complain about, or to be ashamed of. It is a great teacher.

—Dr. Norman Vincent Peale

If you treat a man as he is, he will stay as he is; but, if you treat him as if he were what he ought to be, and could be, he will become that bigger and better man.

—Goethe

Knowledge without wisdom is a load of books on a fool's back.

—Japanese proverb

Hero

by Breanne Crawford, 18

Heroes help us define how we would like to approach decisions and life in general. Breanne created this layout to honor two "ordinary people" she considers heroes. Her journaling describes how these people have influenced her life.

SUPPLIES: Stickers are by Frances Meyer. Font is Times New Roman. Chalk is by Inkadinkado. Definition is from www.dictionary.com.

at the time?" Or "Look at this lady. She must have practiced a long time to be that good! What else do you think she had to do to become that good?"

You can also point out examples in your child's own life—"You did it! All that hard work paid off! You can do a page on all it took to get here!" In essence, this encourages children to become self-fulfilling prophecies—once they decide for themselves what the ideals for various positive character traits are, and begin to recognize these situations, they can strive to bring them more fully into their own lives. By pointing out these examples, your child will also see you as a person who will encourage him to be the best person he can be. Chances are, he will come back for more of this feeling, thus cementing the bond between you.

Why is this theme important?

Children's role models can come from a variety of sources, not all of them of our choosing. In creating scrapbook pages about positive character traits, we equip our children with the ability to recognize those traits in others. For example, when they see strong people, they may realize this is a trait they want for themselves.

Recognizing positive character traits allows them to see where living with integrity can lead in their own lives. Down the road, our children can become people to be admired and emulated. How wonderful it would be for our children to become those role models we now seek for them. It can start with our scrapbooks…

In my children's scrapbooks…

These weren't the easiest layouts to get my kids to do. They take some real guidance and strong encouragement. But I believe they will be better for it. James did pages on the meanings of several positive character traits, and how honesty will help him in his future career field (law). My daughter's were more simple—ways she shows love and fairness to her friends, family and classmates.

He who loses wealth loses much;
He who loses a friend loses more;
He who loses his courage loses all.
—Cervantes

We must use time creatively, in the knowledge that the time is always ripe to do right.
—Dr. Martin Luther King, Jr.

You will not be respected unless you respect yourself.
—Mexican proverb

We all have to live here together. Respect each other and see the best in each other.
—Colin Powell

True courage consists not in flying from the storms of life, but in braving and steering through them with wisdom.
—Hannah Webster Foster

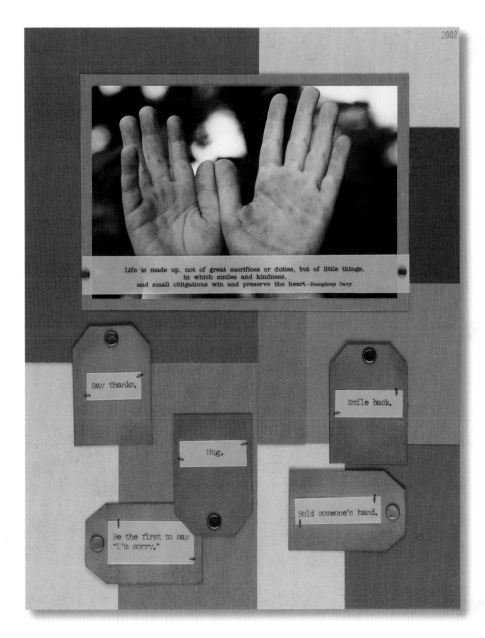

Life is made up, not of great sacrifices or duties, but of little things, in which smiles and kindness, and small obligations win and preserve the heart.—Humphrey Davy

say thanks.

Hug.

Be the first to say "I'm sorry."

Smile back.

Hold someone's hand.

Kindness
by Annie Wheatcraft

Sometimes a special layout about a loved one doesn't have to show their face. This page is about Annie's son and uses a photo of his hands to depict the character traits written in the journaling.

Supplies: Font is Typist. Brads are by Boxer Scrapbook Productions.

You gain strength, courage, and confidence by every experience in which you really stop to look fear in the face.

—Eleanor Roosevelt

To be successful, you must decide exactly what you want to accomplish, then resolve to pay the price to get it.

—Bunker Hunt

Prompts to trigger journaling

☐ Look up the dictionary definitions for several of the positive character traits below, and write them down. Then write about what they mean to you. Journal about a time when you experienced each one in your life, and/or why it's important to act according to that trait.

- o Creativity
- o Respect
- o Responsibility
- o Dedication
- o Empowerment
- o Encouragement
- o Courage
- o Hope
- o Excellence
- o Fairness
- o Faith
- o Friends or friendship
- o Loyalty
- o Compassion
- o Personal Growth
- o Honesty and Integrity
- o Love
- o Patience
- o Perseverance/Determination
- o Confidence
- o Service
- o Trustworthiness

Things I've Learned

← Mistakes happen, that's why there's white-out! ☺

* Santa Claus is real!
* Love at first sight isn't just in fairy tales
* You can do anything you set your mind to.
* "I can do all things through Christ which strengtheneth me." (Phil 4:13)
* School actually does have a purpose!
* Rome wasn't built in a day!
* Trying to hurt others only hurts yourself.
* Love is all you need.
* It's nice to be important, but it's important to be nice.
* "All things work together for good to them that love God, to them who are the called according to His purpose." (Rom. 8:28)
* Don't let your past dictate who you are.
* Prayer changes things.
* Chivalry still exists.
* Classical music really does make you think better!
* True beauty comes from within.
* Money isn't everything.
* God's way is the only way.
* "There hath no temptation taken you but such as is common to man: but God is faithful, who will not suffer you to be tempted above that ye are able, but will with the temptation also make a way to escape, that ye may be able to bear it. (1 Cor. 10:13)
* No one is perfect until you fall in love with them.

* It's the little things in life...
* Take time out to play.
* Trust your intuition!
* Think before speaking.
* Politeness will get you far.
* Smile!
* Learn to laugh at your mistakes.
* Under everyone's hard shell is someone who wants to be loved and appreciated.
* "Trust in the Lord with all thine heart, and lean not unto thine own understanding. In all thy ways acknowledge him, and He shall direct thy paths (Prov. 3:5-6)
* Seek first to understand, then to be understood. (Covey)
* Most likely, what upsets you now won't make any difference later on.
* It's far, far better to give than to receive.
* Dream big!
* Listen to your parents- they really do know best!
* Don't take anyone you love for granted.
* Always, always, always be positive + look for the good in everyone and every situation.

June 2003

Things I've Learned

by Amanda Goodwin, age 16

Using a ruler and Zig pens, Amanda designed two sheets of white cardstock to look like notebook paper. She used a ball-point pen to list things she's learned.

When putting down the letter stickers in the title, she accidentally smudged some black ink below, creating an opportunity to write another life lesson!

SUPPLIES: Paper is by Chatterbox. Stickers are by Making Memories. White out is by Paper Mate.

❑ What does it mean to be a hero? List three famous heroes and why they are famous. You could use tags or slips of paper to record historical trivia for famous people.

❑ Who is your personal hero? What traits do you admire in this person? What have you learned from him or her? You could use tags or slips of paper to record historical trivia for famous people. You could scrap more than one person.

❑ Describe the ways in which your life is rich. Which positive character traits do you possess that help make your life rich? Name one character muscle you might need to strengthen so you can enjoy a richer life at school and at home.

❑ Who do you talk to when you need help or guidance?

❑ Complete this statement: "I wish I could be like [a person's name]. This person is special because…"

❑ What would you do if a bully bothered you on your way home?

❑ What would you do if someone said you did something wrong and you didn't?

❑ What is your advice to those younger than you? What have you learned that you think they should know?

I may disagree with what you have to say, but I shall defend to the death your right to say it.

—Voltaire

A hero is no braver than an ordinary man, but braver five minutes longer. The big question is whether you are going to be able to say a hearty yes to your adventure.

—Joseph Campbell

It's not that I'm so smart, it's just that I stay with problems longer.

—Albert Einstein

Success seems to be connected with action. Successful people keep moving. They make mistakes, but they don't quit.

—Conrad Hilton

Eighty percent of success is showing up.

—Woody Allen

Smile, for everyone lacks self-confidence and more than any other one thing a smile reassures them.

—Andre Maurois

MY TOP 10 CHARACTER TRAITS
Character is what you are in the dark. ~ *Dwight L. Moody*

LEADER
I am a leader: I care about others and I love to serve. I try to set a good example in my family, with my friends, and everywhere I am. I can accept advice and criticism without exploding. If I see a problem, I try to fix it. I want to inspire others to be all that they were created to be.

CREATIVE
I use my imagination to be creative. I love to scrapbook, write, sew, quilt, craft, paint, etc... My mind is a gold mine of creativity.

GENUINE
I am genuine and authentic. I don't bother with masquerades - God made me special and I don't have try to be somebody else. I realize that I'm not perfect; I make mistakes, but that's okay.

RESPONSIBLE
I take responsibility for my own actions and decisions. I am dependable and reliable. I organize my life and honor my commitments. I have a moral responsibility to other people - to defend, care for and help. I am accountable to my family, community, country, and God.

CONFIDENT
It takes confidence to take a stand and speak out against unjustice. I don't care what other people think of me. I'm not afraid to do the right thing. I try my best to succeed, even when things get difficult. When I fail, I can pick myself up and try again. I have confidence to face things that I'm afraid of.

COMPASSIONATE
When someone is hurting, I try to help. I have compassion for others - especially innocent children who are at risk of starvation, disease, war, and abuse.

STRONG
I'm not talking about physical strength, but emotional and spiritual strength. I know who I am and what I believe in. I can stand up to my friends if I know they're doing something wrong. I will not back down in the face of adversity.

LOYAL
I am loyal to my family, friends, and God. I'm also loyal to myself and my principles - I can stick up for myself and for what I know is right.

FRIENDLY
I notice and reach out to other people, especially when they're hurting. I don't focus on myself when I'm with others - I listen and ask questions. I believe that being supportive, respectful, honest, and kind is very important in any relationship.

FOCUSED
I concentrate on things that are important to me, and I am not easily distracted. My biggest problem is that I have too many things that I'm interested in. I like to plan ahead and make goals to be reached. When I start something, I stick to it.

My Top 10 Character Traits
by Natasha Yaceko

Natasha listed what she considers to be her strongest traits. She goes on to describe each trait in detail. A similar layout could also describe specific occasions when a trait was used.

SUPPLIES: Punch is EK Success Paper Shapers spiral. Fonts are a mix of computer fonts.

www.

Definitions of character attributes:
www.charactercenter.com/Definitions/index.htm

Activities for character development:
www.charactercenter.com/act1/index.htm
www.goodcharacter.com
www.wiseskills.com/samples.html
www.storiestogrowby.com/values.html

Parent guides from *The Book of Virtues*:
pbskids.org/adventures/caregivers/parent_guides.html

The "Periodic Table of Behavioral Elements":
www.ourcharacter.com/behavioral.html

Building self-esteem and confidence in children:
www.essortment.com/in/Children.Development/
www.moralintelligence.com/Pages/5buildingBlocks.htm

How to raise kids who stand up for their beliefs:
www.moralintelligence.com/Pages/ArtBMI16.htm

Emotional vocabulary list:
www.moralintelligence.com/Pages/ArtBMI09.htm

Mission builder for teens:
www.franklincovey.com/cgi-bin/teens/teens-msb/part01/

❑ What personality trait do you admire most and why?

❑ What does is mean to show courage? List three ways or times you have been courageous.

❑ Tell about a time when you were honest, even though you were tempted to lie.

❑ List your convictions—what do you believe in?

❑ Using one of the quotes offered in the sidebar, describe when you experienced something similar in your life.

❑ What are some ways you can show respect for your family? Your friends? Strangers or people in your community? Classmates?

❑ Look up the definition of *perseverance*. When have you persevered and accomplished something, even though you wanted to quit?

❑ Who is the most patient person you know? How do you know they are patient? How can you be more like them?

❑ What are the positive character traits of a good leader? Interview your parents, or another adult and ask, "What makes a good leader? Can you think of a leader (either in your school, your community or in government) that is a good leader?"

❑ Write a poem about hope and illustrate it.

Photos to find or request

❑ Photos of hero(es)—famous or from personal life

❑ Photo of a person your children think is brave or courageous

❑ Photos of a volunteer project or charity drive

❑ Photo of your child practicing a skill, like a musical instrument, or handwriting the word *perseverance* or *dedication*

Pictures to take

❑ Photo of homework spread out on a table or a pet's food dish and leash (*responsibility*)

❑ Photo of your child at a race finish line (*perseverance, excellence*)

❑ Photo of someone praying (*faith*)

❑ Photo of your child hugging a loved one (*love*)

❑ Photo of someone they trust (*trustworthiness*)

❑ Photo of someone who encourages them (teacher, coach, minister, etc.)

Mike,

I realize now that I never got the chance to sign your yearbook. I know we were both saving pages in them for each other to write on, but I thought instead of writing in your yearbook, I would make you this page. Hopefully you know by now how much I love you. I know I say "I love you" a lot but a phrase I don't often say is "I am proud of you." And I want you to know that I am proud of you. I am proud of all of your accomplishments throughout the past 3 years, and throughout your life. I am amazed and your knowledge and wisdom. You have such a deep way of thinking and feeling that makes you different from everyone else. You are artistic, creative, and original. You like to try new things, and you like to keep trying until you have found something that is better than your last way of doing it. You are always trying to better yourself in each project you endeavor. You have so much patience and diligence. You are a great example to me to never give up when things get hard. You are also very generous. I think about all the hard work you put into helping Keepsake Corner get everything up and running, and how you edited their ad photos, and offered to make a short movie for them. I think about how you receive so much joy from teaching others, whether it be swing dancing, photography, or computer skills. I know this gift will help you on your mission and throughout the rest of your life. I don't think a person is truly wise until they share their wisdom with others, and that's exactly what you do. You care about people deeply. You look at them and see the beauty within that person. You have faith in people, and you believe in them even when they don't believe in themselves. You always light up a room. You bring a smile to so many people as you make them laugh. Your sense of humor is part of what made me first fall in love with you. You certainly caught my attention with your jokes, but kept me along with your huge heart. I can't imagine a better person to be around for two years. You taught me, challenged me, helped me grow, and most importantly, taught me how to love. Through loving you, I learned how to love myself. Through being with you, I learned how to be myself. I want you to know that no matter what the past was like, or what the future may bring, that you will always be you because of what is within you. It is something that can't be changed. I love you sweetie. Thank you for some of the best years of my life.   Yours Truly, Erica

What lies behind us
and what lies before us
are tiny matters compared to what
lies within us.

What Lies Within Us
by Erica Shaw, age 18

In this heartfelt letter to her boyfriend, Erica spells out exactly what she admires most about him—his knowledge, wisdom, creativity, perseverance, patience and generosity. She cites specific examples of each character trait and how those traits have influenced her as a person.

Supplies: Cardstock is by Pebbles in My Pocket. Fonts are Typewriter, Scriptina and CK Bella. Metal letters are by Making Memories. Dotlets are by Doodlebug.

7: MY PROGRESS

This section helps illustrate skills or areas children may be working to improve.

Just about everything your child does is a Work in Progress—children seem to grow and change every hour, right before our eyes! But there are often areas your child is working on specifically, with intent and focus.

This could be a skill, such as the A-scale on the violin or a skill like that illustrated in Nathan's golf layout on the next page. It could be something behavioral, like using good manners in a restaurant or not speaking out of turn in school. It could be something like improving skills on math story problems or being better about sharing toys (always a tough one).

Your role in all this is to encourage kids to document this process. Point out their Works in Progress —"I've noticed you seem to spend a lot of time on your algebra homework," or, "You seem to be frustrated after your violin lessons; you're working so hard at getting better."

Suggest that you come up with a plan of action together. Put yourself in the role of cheerleader, and your child is more likely to return to you for support and advice in the future. And, if you help guide them through scrapbooking about these things, you're reinforcing to them that you believe in persistence and the rewards it brings.

Dance and Me
by Kelcie Thomas, age 12

Kelcie created this layout to document how her dance skills are a Work in Progress. She also included her next dance-related goal.

SUPPLIES: Paper is by Paper Adventures. Title font is Curlz; journaling font is Bernhard Modern Roman. Ribbon is by Close to My Heart.

Dance and ME

I have loved to dance since I was little, but it takes a lot of work and dedication. I've gone from running around the stage to leaps and turns in only a few years. I am really proud of myself. My next goal is to make the tri-del dance/drill team in 2 years.

Debbie DeMars came up with a neat way to encourage her son to document his Work in Progress —his golf skills. She created a list of questions in a worksheet format so he could provide answers in his own handwriting. Here are the questions she included:

❑ What goal are you working toward?

❑ Why do you want to do it?

❑ How old are you?

❑ How old do you think you'll be when you reach your goal?

❑ What do you need to work on to make it happen?

❑ What will it look like when you reach your goal? (Here she left room for him to draw a picture.)

Why is this theme important?

Persistence is a hard lesson! When we encourage kids to document what they're working on, we allow them to take ownership of what they're learning on their own. They can, in essence, say, "This is something I'm working on. This is something I want for myself."

Once they recognize that a skill or concept is a good and useful thing, they are more likely to want to work towards that goal. And once they see it as a goal of their own—rather than one imposed on them by an adult—it becomes more palatable.

Documenting goals, and the process of achieving goals, also provides kids with a framework with which

You have powers you never dreamed of. You can do things you never thought you could do. There are no limitations to what you can do except the limitations of your own mind.

—Darwin P. Kingsley

I Love Golf
by Nathan DeMars, age 6

Nathan's mom created a worksheet of questions to guide his journaling. Consider using a similar worksheet to help your children document their activities.

Supplies: Markers are by Zig.

to attack future challenges. They can remind themselves, "When I chose to be a better pitcher, I had to practice every day for a whole summer!" It not only reminds them that most skills take dedication and hard work, but also that practicing does pay off. Having a plan for achieving goals helps speed the process along.

In my children's scrapbooks...

My son did a page on nightmares he used to have and another on his speech classes, including his graduation from the class. He also did a page on how hard it is to practice new things on the violin but how much he likes playing a song he's learned. I plan to encourage my daughter to do a page on learning to take constructive criticism without crying. For this, we will need to develop a plan of action together!

Prompts to trigger journaling

❑ What are you afraid of? Draw a picture of something that you are afraid of.

❑ Write about a time when you were very frightened. How did you get over it?

❑ Make a list of things you would like to learn to do.

❑ Complete this statement: I wish I had one more chance to…. Then I would be able to….

I became involved in track in 2002, my seventh grade year. Going into track, I was a little unsure of myself because I heard it was hard and I thought I wasn't going to be as good as everyone else. But that season changed my thoughts on running. I enjoyed it a lot. I worked hard at getting better and it made me feel good about myself. I thought it was really fun and I didn't care if I didn't win a race, I was doing it for my personal best. For ME to improve, and for me to get in better shape. But what I didn't know was, that season I was going to get first in all the mile races. I also didn't know that I was going to set the school's Girls's Mile record, with a time of 6.07. Then this year, in eighth grade track I progressed and I still hold the record and hope to hold it for quite a while..

- What is the most adventurous thing you have ever done?

- When were you the most proud of yourself?

- When were your parents very proud of you? Have them write a letter to you about that time and include it in your scrapbook.

- Who do you talk to when you have a problem?

- What is something you dislike about yourself? How could you change it?

- Think of something you'd like to improve about yourself at school, home or with your friends. What would it be?

- What is something that really makes you angry? Do you have trouble controlling your anger? What could you do differently when you get angry?

- What's the best self-improvement advice you've ever gotten? Who gave it to you? How did it make you a better person?

- Sometimes we don't try things because someone tells us it's too hard or we won't be good at it. What would you like to try anyway?

- What are some thoughts that you often think about yourself that aren't positive? How can you change those thoughts?

The world will change for the better when people decide they are sick and tired of being sick and tired of the way the world is, and decide to change themselves.

—Sidney Madwed

Aren't you tired of doing what you already know how to do?

—Pam Grout

Track Star
by Meredith Parks, age 14

Meredith's journaling describes how her running is a Work in Progress. She journals her thoughts and feelings throughout her two years on the track team. She also lists milestones and accomplishments she's achieved while working to improve her skills.

Layouts on Works in Progress can illustrate any number of topics—areas where improvement is needed, in progress or even partially completed.

Supplies: Patterned paper is by Scrappin' Dreams. Cardstock is by Making Memories. Journaling font is Childish (www.onescrappysite.com). Letters for title cut with Accucut ShapeMaker Template. Finish line posts are Meredith's own design.

If you want to be successful, find someone who has achieved the results you want and copy what they do and you'll achieve the same results.

—Anthony Robbins

Twenty years from now you will be more disappointed by the things that you didn't do than by the ones you did do. So throw off the bowlines. Sail away from the safe harbor. Catch the trade winds in your sails. Explore. Dream. Discover.

—Mark Twain

Something I Would Change & Memory Box
by Mikel "Tiffany" Gill

This is a project that Tiffany completed for her Sociology of the Family class. Her requirements were to explore family relationships and to understand how who she is today will influence her life and career choices in the next few years.

This particular page includes Tiffany's thoughts on what she would like to change about herself to improve relationships. She found the box at a variety store just after Easter. She cut up posterboard to make the pages so that they would be sturdy enough to withstand being taken in and out of the box.

SUPPLIES: Posterboard and ribbon. Font is Times New Roman.

❑ How do you feel when something is very difficult for you to do? Do you give up or keep trying? Why?

❑ If you are trying to improve something in your life, why do you want it to get better?

❑ What's something you wish your mother or father would improve?

❑ Explain how you could get better at something.

❑ Think of someone who's already good at something you'd like to do. Name that person and why you think they're so good. What advice do you think they would give you?

❑ Draw a picture of yourself after you've achieved your goal.

Photos to find or request

❑ Photo of your child at a lesson or practice

❑ Photo of your child doing homework

❑ Photo of your child reading helpful magazines or books

❑ Photo of something before you improved it (a messy room or something like a skinned knee from falling during a practice)

❑ Photo of your child receiving an award for accomplishing their goal

Pictures to take

❑ Photo of someone who's already good at the chosen Work in Progress

❑ Photo of a teacher or coach is helping your child improve

❑ Photo a practice session

❑ Photo (or drawing) of what the child is afraid of

❑ Photo of elements of a Work in Progress (sports equipment, musical instruments, textbooks, homework, toys, etc).

Nightmares

by James Pedersen, age 8

This layout demonstrates the fun kids can have with scrapbooking. James giggled for 20 minutes straight while putting this page together—even though it was a potentially serious topic. For his page design, stickers were obviously a favorite choice, followed by paper dolls.

For Work in Progress pages, it can often be easier to take a light-hearted approach to areas in which your child may be struggling. The journaling can still point out what your child is working on.

SUPPLIES: Patterned paper is by NRN Designs. Stickers are by SandyLion, Mrs. Grossman's and Frances Meyer. Diecut is by Accu-Cut. Decorative scissors are by Fiskars. Paper piecing is James' own design.

This page is about my nightmares. Sometimes I get freaky nightmares. I can barely sleep. I like these freaky skeletons because they're not scary—they're funny. And if I think of something funny, I'm not so scared

www.

Coping strategies:
www.eduplace.com/
activity/rough.html

Help kids embrace change:
www.teachervision.com/
lesson-plans/lesson-
21093.html
www.eduplace.com/
activity/gears.html

11 quizzes to help kids get to know themselves:
feteens.com/WhoAmI/
index_en-US.html

Focus on kids' progress:
www.decatursports.com/
articles/kidsprogress.htm

Document progress:
www.suntimes.com/
education/learn/
conf1.html

Progress report for preschoolers:
www.atozkidsstuff.com/
prereport1.html

Helping your child series:
www.ed.gov/pubs/
parents/hyc.html

Positive thinking for kids:
www.atozkidsstuff.com/
article6.html

Supporting of growth:
www.atozkidsstuff.com/
article29.html

Raising confident girls:
www.parentsandgirls.
com/

Motivational quotes:
www.getmotivation.com/
favorites.html

Something I would change about me...

I think the one thing I would change would be getting people to trust me easier. I have been told by one of really good friends that I am hard to trust. He isn't really sure why, but he says it has something to do with the fact that I get along a lot better with guys and that I can just talk to anyone for hours about any problems or anything and that it causes a problem for him because he wouldn't want to lose me to anyone else, so I would want to change the fact that I'm not easy to trust.

I would change that by spending more time with the people I care about more and not blow them off, also by telling them more about how I feel, and explaining that I'm just an over friendly person and that I love attention.

8: MY DAYDREAMS

This section is about exploring possibilities. It's about encouraging your child to put himself or herself into the future and imagine what kind of life they might have.

One thing I've always admired and appreciated about children is that their minds and imaginations aren't tainted by thoughts like, "Oh, that would never work," or "I could never do that" or "I'm not very creative."

Children often possess the confidence that whatever they dream up can happen. It's our job as the influential adults in their lives to encourage these dreams and to encourage them to explore every avenue that these dreams can offer.

If your child has trouble imagining possibilities, you can guide him with questions until he is able to begin to dream. Then your child can commit those dreams to scrapbook layouts.

In scrapping pages within this theme, I suggest you encourage your child to put himself or herself into the future and imagine what kind of life they will be living. Guide him or her in journaling about future jobs, homes, and lifestyles—what will their life be like 10 years from now? 20 years from now?

Once they have some ideas on where they might like to be, they have a chance to perhaps figure out how to get there. They can create their own action plans of steps they need to take to achieve those goals.

Someday
by Jackie Rice

How many times have you heard your child say, "Someday, I'll..."? The end of that statement seems to change weekly, sometimes daily! Encourage children to jot down those dreams or jot them down yourself.

Jackie made it easy to do a layout featuring dreams—just write them on cardstock and sprinkle them on bright background paper. No need for pictures! Be sure to note the date so that you can keep track of the "dreamer" and the dreams.

SUPPLIES: Patterned paper is by SEI. Font is 2Ps Ribbons (www.twopeasinabucket.com). Hand lettering is by Jackie.

Breaking down long-term goals into manageable steps is a very necessary skill, both in higher education and in the business world.

A scrapbook is a great place to explore fantastic possibilities —address all the "what-if's" that may be ever-present in your child's mind. I know my son presents me daily with "what-if's". What if cars were free? What car would you get? What if we only ate desserts? What would happen? What if I don't clean my room? What will happen then?

He loves to consider possibilities and I wholeheartedly encourage that. (I also encourage him to clean his room, so we don't have to find out what happens if he doesn't…)

In an article at mi.essortment.com, Jeanette Scharsch writes, "Let them dare to dream. Guide them in identifying where they want to go in life. Get them to dream about the possibilities that are out there.

"Ask questions like, 'What do you want to do this year in football or academics?', or 'Where do you want to be 10 years from now?' Then allow them to let their thoughts roam. Let them visualize themselves living out their dreams.

"When they come to you with a vision, you are ready to take the next important step." You can work with them on goal-setting and action plans, or you can just see where their dreams take them, just for the fun of dreaming."

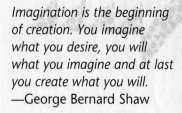

Imagination is the beginning of creation. You imagine what you desire, you will what you imagine and at last you create what you will.
—George Bernard Shaw

Childhood Dreams / I'm Still Dreaming
by Breanne Crawford, age 18

It's always interesting to see which dreams change and which ones stay the same. Breanne typed up her journaling, printed it out on vellum and sliced it up. This "then and now" approach makes a very doable layout!

SUPPLIES: Patterned paper is by ProvoCraft. Vellum is by DMD Industries.

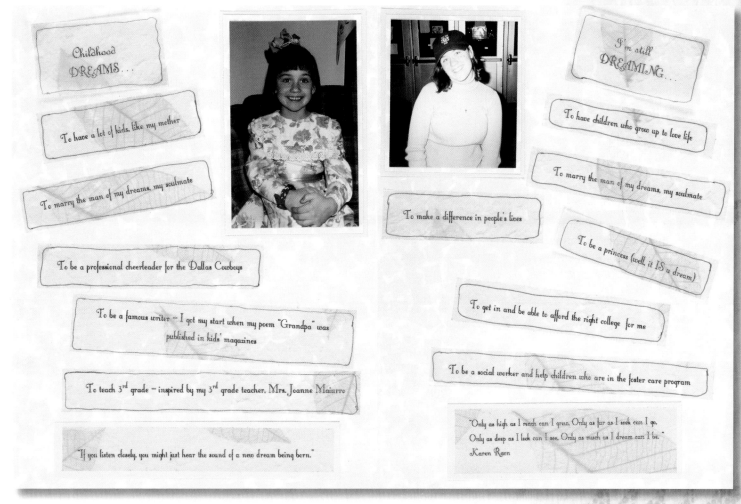

Childhood DREAMS…

To have a lot of kids, like my mother

To marry the man of my dreams, my soulmate

To be a professional cheerleader for the Dallas Cowboys

To be a famous writer — I got my start when my poem "Grandpa" was published in kids' magazines

To teach 3rd grade — inspired by my 3rd grade teacher, Mrs. Joanne Maiurro

"If you listen closely, you might just hear the sound of a new dream being born."

I'm still DREAMING…

To have children who grow up to love life

To marry the man of my dreams, my soulmate

To make a difference in people's lives

To be a princess (well, it IS a dream)

To get in and be able to afford the right college for me

To be a social worker and help children who are in the foster care program

"Only as high as I reach can I grow, Only as far as I seek can I go. Only as deep as I look can I see, Only as much as I dream can I be."
Karen Ravn

One of the greatest weaknesses in most of us is our lack of faith in ourselves.
—L. Tom Perry

A man's dreams are an index to his greatness.
—Zadok Rabinwitz

My hopes are not always realized, but I always hope.
—Ovid

The secret of all those who make discoveries is that they regard nothing as impossible.
—Justus Liebig

The future belongs to those who believe in the beauty of their dreams.
—Eleanor Roosevelt

Discovery consists of looking at the same thing as everyone else and thinking something different.
—Albert Szent-Gyorgyi

My Secret Power

by Joanne Pedersen, age 5

One of the neat things about kids is their ability to image seemingly impossible things. In this layout, Joanne describes what she wishes were her "secret powers." She drew her version of the creature—complete with butterfly-turtle sidekick!. Joanne indicated why she would like to have this power: So sometimes she wouldn't feel shy.

SUPPLIES: Coloring pencils are by EK Success.

Why is this theme important?

Daydreaming (also called brainstorming) is the first step in critical thinking and creative problem solving.

You cannot come up with the most effective solution to a problem unless you can consider all the possible approaches to a suitable end result. By encouraging creative thinking in our children, we are, in essence, teaching them the skills they need to be effective thinkers and problem-solvers.

We are also fostering in them the conviction that their ideas—no matter how fantastic—have merit and can be achievable. Doing a page on "your favorite secret power" might seem frivolous as a teaching tool, but when your child considers a topic like that, they are also digging into their own wells of creativity to figure out a way around physical limitations. Those creative resources will serve them well throughout their lives.

In my children's scrapbooks...

My son did a page on his current "when-I-grow-up" job—he wants to be a lawyer. He journaled about how much he would make, where he would live, how much schooling he would need, and what kind of lawyer he would be. My son also did a layout about all the fantastic

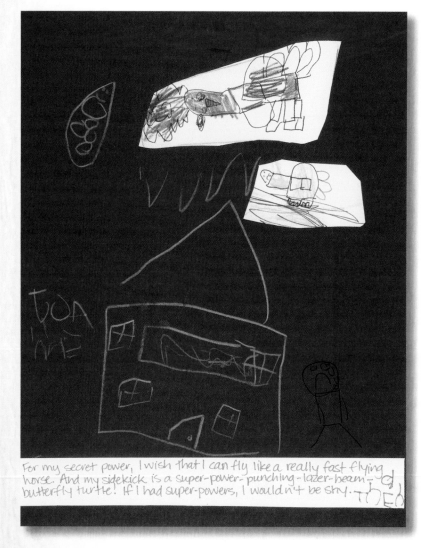

For my secret power, I wish that I can fly like a really fast flying horse. And my sidekick is a super-power-punching-lazer-beam-butterfly turtle! If I had super-powers, I wouldn't be shy.

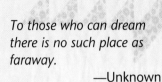

creatures he draws. I wanted my daughter to do a page about her future career as a "crime-fighting veterinarian", but her goals changed too quickly to catch it for her own book, so it may have to go in the family album! She chose to do a page on her favorite secret power.

Prompts to trigger journaling

❑ Describe your goals and dreams for when you grow up. What job will you have? Will you be married? Where will you live? What will you do in your spare time?

❑ Draw a picture of what you want to be when you grow up.

❑ How will you know if you are successful when you grow up?

❑ What are the top 10 things you want to do in your lifetime? And how can you make those things happen?

❑ What would happen if you found gold in your backyard?

❑ What would you do if you found a magic wand? What would be your first wish granted or first spell cast?

❑ If you could have been a famous person in history, who would you have been? Why? Include some biographical information on that person.

❑ If you could participate in an Olympic event, which one would you choose and why? Research some medalists from that event.

To those who can dream there is no such place as faraway.
—Unknown

Imagination: The ability to confront and deal with reality by using the creative power of the mind; resourcefulness.
—The American Heritage® Dictionary

Imagination gathers up The undiscovered Universe, Like jewels in a jasper cup.
—John Davidson

Bella Bambinaz
by Valeria Chiappetta

Val saw a need for an all-girl promotion company and, together with friends, started their own company. They took their dream of "making a difference in a male-dominated industry," and made it a reality. Val included memorabilia from their promotional events in the pocket she created behind the photo.

SUPPLIES: Stickers are Jolee's Star Corners. Journaling font is Enviro.

I dream of vague shapes that hint of my heart's desire.
— Mason Cooley

Imagination is the voice of daring. If there is anything Godlike about God it is that. He dared to imagine everything.

— Henry Miller

To come to be you must have a vision of Being, a Dream, a Purpose, a Principle. You will become what your vision is.
— Peter Nivio Zarlenga

To accomplish great things, we must dream as well as act.

— Anatole France

❏ If you could be in the *Guinness Book of World Records*, what would your record be? See if someone already has that record—what would you have to do to beat?

❏ If you could have any superpower, what would it be? Draw a picture of yourself using your superpower.

❏ If you could have the answer to any question, what question would you ask? To whom would you ask it?

❏ If you could invent one thing to improve your life, what would it be? How much would it cost?

❏ If you could be any animal for a day, what animal would you choose? Why? What would you do that day? Draw a picture of yourself as that animal.

❏ Complete this statement: I wish there really was _____. If there really was _____, then.....

❏ What do you want to do after you graduate from high school?

❏ What is the weirdest dream you've ever had?

❏ What are your fears, expectations and anticipations about getting married?

❏ What would you give yourself if money were no object? What would you give your family?

Travel Dreams
by Rachel Yaceyko, age 12

Rachel has big dreams— look at all the places she'd like to visit! Her journaling reveals her thought process for defining how she could make those dreams come true. Rachel made this layout more personal by mentioning specific family members and their role in her job search.

To make a similar layout, ask your child what destinations they would like to travel to. Then have them draw a picture to include on the layout.

SUPPLIES: *Journaling font is Arial.*

United States   Liberia   Bermuda   Belguim   Rwanda   Ethiopia
Romania   Peru   AFGHANISTAN   Morocco   Austria   Finland   Israel
Venezuela   Sweden   Colombia   Turkey   Japan   Chad   Egypt
Philippines   Kenya   Saudi Arabia   Pakistan   Ireland   RUSSIA   Haiti

I have loved traveling as far back as I can remember (although my stomach disagrees). It wasn't until a year ago (2002), I decided I wanted to do lots of traveling.

One night I was talking to my Dad, telling him where I wanted to travel. I guess I had been talking awhile because he asked me where I didn't want to travel. I couldn't think of anywhere I didn't want to go, other than to Antartica (brrr)!

I was hoping when I get older that I will be able to visit a couple of countries, but then one night, I was thinking about it and thought "what if I get a job where I travel" ~ a trucker, flight attendant, etc... Even if I was traveling around Canada and the United States, I would be just as happy!

I have had a couple of talks with Auntie Rebecca, Mandy and Rae (along with Auntie Joc and Uncle Lorne) about it, and they have helped me come up with quite a few jobs I could do while traveling. Uncle Lorne is a trucker and has a ball traveling around. Mandy and Rae (his daughters) have gone on a couple of trips with him and have a wonderful time traveling the country and seeing all the different towns, cities, and landmarks.

POLAND   New Zealand   Canada   France   ARGENTINA   INDIA
Indonesia   Ecuador   Greece   HONG KONG   China
Germany   Thailand   PUERTO RICO   Ukraine   Mexico   Spain
Cuba   Bahamas   HUNGARY   Brazil   Jamaica   Costa Rica   Honduras
Australia   El Salvador   Italy   Netherlands   Nepal

- If you won $100 million in the lottery:
  - o What are five things you would purchase for yourself? Include the approximate price of each item.
  - o What are five things you would purchase for others? For whom would you buy these gifts?
  - o For what would you save money? Would you invest any of the money or donate money to a charity? To which charity?
- Interview an adult your are close to about your future—what does that adult think you might be doing in 10 to 20 years? In what field does he or she think you can excel? Have the adult make some predictions about you.

- To what place would you like to travel? What you would see, do and eat once you got there. Whom would you take with you? Draw a picture of what you might see on your travels or find some pictures on the Internet.

- If you were famous, what would you be famous for? How would your life be different?

- George Seaton said, "The imagination is a place all by itself. A separate country. Now, you've heard of the French nation, the British nation. Well, this is the Imagi-nation. It's a wonderful place." Draw a picture of what "Imagi-nation" looks like.

The imagination is a place all by itself. A separate country. Now, you've heard of the French nation, the British nation. Well, this is the Imagi-nation. It's a wonderful place.
—George Seaton

Imagination has rules, but we can only guess what they are.
—Mason Cooley

Children love to be alone because alone is where they know themselves, and where they dream.
—Roger Rosenblatt

... the imagination needs moodling,—long, inefficient, happy idling, dawdling and puttering.
—Barbara Ueland

What a glorious gift is imagination, and what satisfaction it affords!
—Thomas Mann

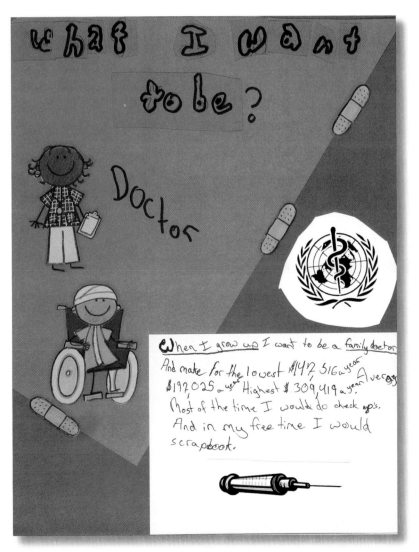

What I Want To Be
by Laura Laue, age 10

Laura included very specific job details in her journaling, such as lowest, average and highest salary! She also describes what she would do at her job and during her spare time. When you come up with specifics for your daydreams, they begin the transition into plans and goals.

SUPPLIES: Cardstock is by Serendipity Papers, Stickers are by Me & My Big Ideas. Clipart from the Internet. Hand lettering is by Laura.

WWW.

Inspiring ideas from Crayola:
www.crayola.com/ideas/index.cfm?mt=ideas

Create a "wish bank":
www.badgerland.co.uk/education/projects/kidsprojects.html

Neat lesson plan on writing a poem about your "secret power":
www.twc.org/forums/writers_on_teaching/fwir_nhefner.html

Goal-setting activities for kids:
www.activityvillage.co.uk/goal_setting_for_kids.htm

Celebrate National Kids' Goal-Setting Week:
www.goalsguy.com/Events/k-celebrate.html

Helping kids become "Goal-Getters":
preteenagerstoday.com/resources/articles/goalgetters.htm

The North Star: an online story dedicated to "those who were brave enough to follow their dreams":
www.fablevision.com/northstar/read/index.html

Photos to find or request

❑ A picture of your child in dress-up clothes

❑ A picture of your child drawing or otherwise using their imagination

❑ A picture of your child pretending to fly, or using some other "secret power"

Pictures to take

❑ Pictures of places your child would like to travel to (from the Internet, brochures, etc.)

❑ A picture of the college campus your child would like to attend

❑ A picture representing something your child wants to accomplish

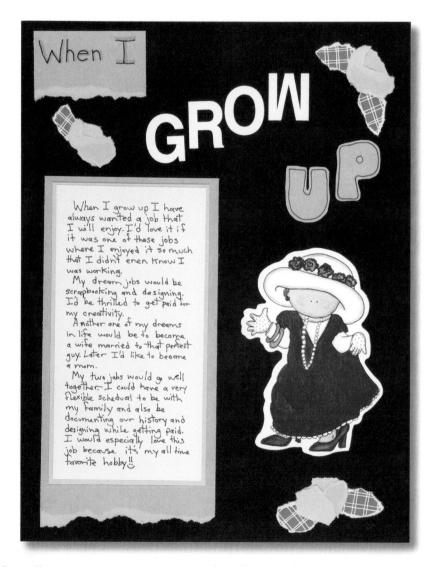

When I Grow Up
by Jolene Belanger, age 14

Jolene's journaling leads you through what she's thinking about for her future. Her words give a sense of her priorities (family and using her creativity), no matter what job she ends up with. Also note the flower embellishments—Jolene created these with scraps of paper.

SUPPLIES: Patterned paper is by Mustard Moon. Cardstock is by Serendipity Papers. Die cuts are by My Mind's Eye. Hand lettering is by Jolene.

When I Grow Up
by Trista Jernigan, age 14

Here, Trista used stickers in place of photos. Her journaling describes a possible future career field and why she's interested in that field.

SUPPLIES: Stickers are by Me & My Big Ideas. Hand lettering is by Trista.

When I Grow Up
by Joyce Belanger, age 10

This girl has some plans! Joyce listed four possible roles for her future and some reasons why they would be a good fit for her. Also, note how she "grounded" the journaling box and the die cut with the same color cardstock and then matted her photo in a different color to make it stand out.

SUPPLIES: Cardstock is by Serendipity Papers. Stickers are by Deja Views. Die cuts are by My Mind's Eye. Hand lettering is by Joyce.

9: MY SPIRITUAL LIFE

Children are born with an innate sense of spirituality because they can find joy and wonder in the simplest of things.

Children often experience these things spontaneously, unconsciously and naturally. When viewed this way, spirituality can inspire layouts on the joy felt in nature and the security felt in the love of one's family. These things can allow deep and abiding feelings of connection and "rightness" in the heart.

As children grow, they often participate in more structured religious activities. They spend time reading and studying religious texts, listening to religious elders and serving those who need help. Everything they hear, learn and experience can influence them on their future spiritual path. If they take the time to document their thoughts on the Divine, and spiritual topics in general, it might help them define what makes the most sense for them. They can also celebrate what they've come to believe about their role in a greater plan.

The Random House Dictionary defines *spirit* as "divine influence as an agency working in the heart of

What I Believe
by Erica Shaw, age 18

Erica based this layout on Joseph Smith's original Articles of Faith. In it, she describes what she believes to be true. Taking time to do this helps clarify a child's spiritual beliefs, as well as lending confidence to those beliefs once they are spelled out on paper.

SUPPLIES: Patterned paper is Sonnets by Creative Imaginations. Striped paper is All About Me by Pebbles in My Pocket. Title fonts are CK Sketch and Wendy Medium. Journaling font is P22 Garamouche. Brads and eylets are by Making Memories.

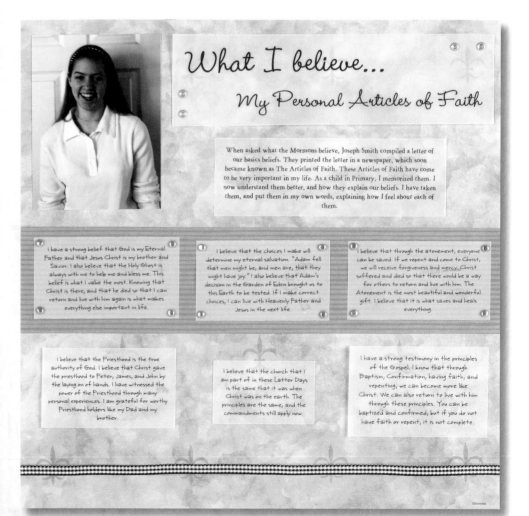

man"; spirituality is "a predominantly spiritual character as shown in thoughts or actions." Children can create pages on how they feel "divine influence" working in their hearts and how this is shown in their thoughts or actions.

They can also explore the teachings of different religions to find the best "fit" for them or how the religion they currently practice feeds their spiritual needs. See Erica Shaw's "Articles of Faith" below for just such a layout. Children can use the prompts on page 63 to explore what they think about God, what prayers or hymns give them comfort and what gives them a sense of peace. Or, they can create pages on subjective, abstract topics such as faith, hope, unconditional love and service.

Homeschooling mother Jill Lazuka shared these thoughts about scrapping the spiritual side of childhood: "Since scrapbooking is a great way to materialize the things you've learned...about yourself, your world, your idea of God ... scrapbooking spirituality encourages children to seriously consider the experiences that they've had. Scrapping their favorite religious story can give them a better understanding of it and it may become a lesson they will remember and share with others. Scrapped verses or songs can serve as spiritual markers and can show children how much they've grown.

If I could sit across the porch from God, I'd thank Him for starry skies, and for walks in the rain. I'd thank Him for friends and family, and for the dreams we dream. If I could sit across the porch from God, I'd thank Him for all the wonder found in this miraculous journey we call life.

—Flavia

I will praise thee for I am fearfully and wonderfully made; your works are wonderful, I know that full well.

—Psalm 139:14

I try to avoid looking forward or backward, and try to keep looking upward.

—Charlotte Bronte

Forever will little opportunities to love daily drop into our hands to abundantly satisfy the question, "Lord, what will you have me do?"

—Unknown

I believe in the sun even when it's not shining. I believe in love even when not feeling it. I believe in God even when He is silent.

—Unknown

We are cups, constantly and quietly being filled. The trick is knowing how to tip ourselves over and let the Beautiful Stuff out.

—Ray Bradbury

Be really whole and all things will come to you.

—Lao Tzu

I believe that God reveals important things pertaining to his Gospel here on the earth through his prophets. I have a testimony that Gordon B. Hinckley is a prophet of God and the things he tells us will help us in this life and the next. I am grateful for the revelation that God will continue to give us throughout time.

I believe that one day we will have an opportunity to live on the earth (which will be renewed) with Christ in the Millenium. I look forward to the day when I can live in Zion and to enjoy the beauty of the restored earth.

I believe in the Bible and the Book of Mormon to be the word of God. I believe that the Book of Mormon is another testament of Jesus Christ. Reading these two books has taught me more than ever. I have come to know Christ through these books. The testimonies of others come into my heart when I read them, and I can better understand the principles I should be living my life by.

I believe in following the laws of the land. Even though sometimes I may not agree with all the laws, I still will follow them and obey and honor the leaders of my country.

I believe that one day we will have an opportunity to live on the earth (which will be renewed) with Christ in the Millenium. I look forward to the day when I can live in Zion and to enjoy the beauty of the restored earth.

I believe that everyone has the right to worship how they may. I am grateful for the opportunity I have to worship freely. I am grateful to live in a country that allows me to worship how I want, and to believe what I want.

There are many miracles that happen in this life, and I believe in them, and that they come from God. God brings revelation and visions to his prophets. I have witnessed many missionaries being able to speak new languages in such a short matter of time, because the spirit is with them to help them preach the Gospel in many tongues.

I believe in being honest and true. I believe that anything that is good and beautiful is of God. I seek after the things in this world that are virtuous. I try to be the best person I can be by remembering this.

"Be thou an Example of the Believers..."

*When you come to the edge of all the light you know, and are about to step off into the darkness of the unknown, faith is knowing one of two things will happen:
There will be something solid to stand on, or you will be taught how to fly.*

—Barbara J. Winter

God is our refuge and strength, a very present help in trouble.

—Psalms 46

"Upon review, those markers become a source of strength and encouragement. Scrapbooking their prayer requests and answers to prayer can add a fun and practical element to the spiritual discipline that kids can enjoy. Scrapbooking religious schools or classes, camp, Baptism or Confirmation, and other religious activities is a great way for children to get excited about spiritual pursuits and to get them to start thinking of the part that they can play in their family's place of workshop, both now and in the future."

Why is this theme important?

When children spend time exploring their own spirituality, they may come to feel a sense of connection to a greater whole. That feeling of connection influences their future decisions and how they interact with others.

When kids feel like they are a part of a greater whole, they may experience a sense of worth and personal responsibility; they may feel they are here for a reason and have a duty to play out. They may see that others around them also have a part to play and may need their support to fulfill their part.

Scrapbooking about spiritual topics and defining their own place in the world can help answer questions children have and provide a sense of belonging and peace.

Young Apostles
by Breanne Crawford, age 18

Breanne used a copy of the Franciscan University Conference website in her journaling. For layouts about your child's youth group experiences, consider using similar details—a definition of the group, what they do together and what topics they typically discuss.

Supplies: Stickers are by Making Memories. Journaling font is Times New Roman. Stencil is by EK Success.

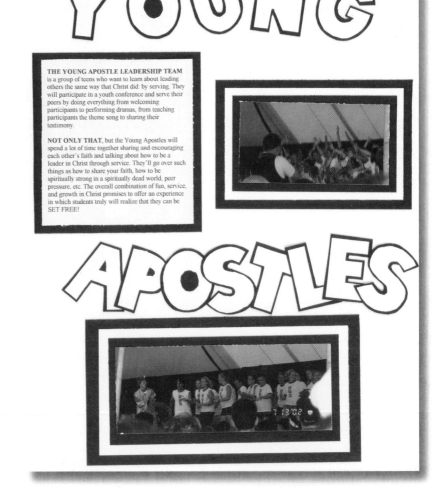

1. YOUNG APOSTLES

THE YOUNG APOSTLE LEADERSHIP TEAM is a group of teens who want to learn about leading others the same way that Christ did: by serving. They will participate in a youth conference and serve their peers by doing everything from welcoming participants to performing dramas, from teaching participants the theme song to sharing their testimony.

NOT ONLY THAT, but the Young Apostles will spend a lot of time together sharing and encouraging each other's faith and talking about how to be a leader in Christ through service. They'll go over such things as how to share your faith, how to be spiritually strong in a spiritually dead world, peer pressure, etc. The overall combination of fun, service, and growth in Christ promises to offer an experience in which students truly will realize that they can be SET FREE!

In my children's scrapbooks...

My son did a layout on Vacation Bible School and some of the lessons he learned there. He may also do a layout on questions he'd like to ask God. My daughter wants to create pages on her favorite parable and "things that are pretty that God has made."

Prompts to trigger journaling

❑ Who or what is God to you? What do you think God looks like? What does God do? Do you use another word for God?

❑ What is your favorite scripture? What does it make you feel or think? Draw a picture of the story, if there is one.

❑ What spiritual writings give you comfort when you're struggling or feeling down?

❑ Do you have a favorite hymn or spiritual song? What do you like about it?

❑ Tell the story of a favorite historical religious figure. What do you like about the story?

❑ What would happen if you loved your neighbor as yourself? What if everyone did?

❑ Describe a time when you felt the spirit very strongly.

❑ Do you believe God has a plan for you? Do you know what it is? How can you find out? Who can you talk to about this?

Now faith is the substance of things hoped for, the evidence of things not seen.
—The Epistle of Paul the Apostle to the Hebrews

I tell you these things that you may learn wisdom; that you may learn that when you are in the service of your fellow beings you are only in the service of your God.
—Church of Jesus Christ of Latter-day Saints. Book of Mormon, Mosiah 2.17

Let all that you do be done with love.
—I Corinthians 16:14

JOYFUL JOYFUL WE ADORE THEE

Joyful, joyful we adore Thee,
God of glory, Lord of love;
Hearts unfold like flowers before Thee,
Hail Thee as the sun above.
Melt the coulds of sin and sadness,
Drive the dark of doubt away;
Giver of immortal gladness,
Fill us with the light of day!

All Thy works with joy surround Thee,
Earth and heaven reflect Thy rays,
Stars and angels sing around Thee,
Center of unbroken praise;
Field and forest, vale and mountain,
Bloss'ming meadow, flashing sea,
Chanting bird and flowing fountain
Call us to rejoice in Thee.

Thou art giving and forgiving,
Ever blessing, ever blest,
Well-spring of the joy of living,
Ocean depth of happy rest!
Thou the Father, Christ our Brother –
All who live in love are Thine;
Teach us how to love each other,
Lift us to the joy divine.

Mortals, join the mighty chorus
Which the morning stars began;
Father love is reigning o'er us,
Brother love binds man to man.
Ever singing we march onward,
Victors in the midst of strife;
Joyful music lifts us sunward
In the triumph song of life!

For as long as I can remember, I have loved the hymn "Joyful, joyful". When I hear it sung or played, I feel uplifted. In the movie Sister Act II, high school students do a version of this song for a singing competition that is absolutely awesome! When I started taking piano lessons, "Joyful, joyful" was the first song I taught myself. That way I could play it for myself whenever I was feeling depressed. My favorite part is the second half of the last verse.

Ludwig van Beethoven (1770-1827) composed this tune, "Hymn to Joy", when he was completely deaf. It is the final movement of his last and greatest symphony, the Ninth Symphony. When this symphony was first performed in 1824, the musicians had to turn Beethoven around so that he could see the thunderous ovation from the audience.

The lyrics to this song were written by Henry van Dyke (1852-1933) while he was visiting Williams College in Massachusetts. He was a respected theologian, a Presbyterian minister, a Navy chaplain during World War I, a professor of literature at Princeton University, and also an ambassador to Holland for a short time.

Joyful, Joyful We Adore Thee
by Natasha Yaceko, age 16

Natasha's journaling is very important here since there are no photos. She talks about what the hymn means to her as well as including historical information. What a unique insight for Natasha to pass on to future generations.

Supplies: Patterned paper is by Scrapbook Sally. Vellum is by WorldWin Extraordinary Papers. Button angel stamp is by Hero Arts. Alphabet punches are by Marvy. Eyelets are by Making Memories.

Prayer is not asking. It is a longing of the soul.
      —Mohandas Ghandi

NAMASTE'—The spirit in me greets the spirit in you. I bow to the Divine in you; I honor the place in you that is of love, truth and light. And when you are in that place in you and I am in that place in me, We Are One.
      —An Ancient Sanskrit Greeting

❑ Write down things you believe are true. (This is your testimony.)

❑ How do you practice your faith in your home?

❑ What brings you eace and why?

❑ What do you pray for or about? Write about how a prayer has been answered.

❑ How do you feel about death? What do you believe happens to people when they die?

❑ Do you currently go to a church, synagogue, mosque or another religious group? What are your worship services like? What do you like best?

❑ What is your favorite religious holiday? What's your favorite part of that holiday?

❑ What does "faith" mean to you?

❑ Do you believe in angels? What do you think they look like? What do you think they do?

❑ What are you thankful for? Do you keep a gratitude journal?

❑ If you could ask God five questions, what would they be? What conversation would you like to have with God?

Living the Life
by Christina Foran, age 16

Over the years, Christina has taken hundreds of photos. She picked some of her favorites from her collection to use in this layout and combined them with relevant Bible verses that have impacted her life.

SUPPLIES: Patterned paper is by ProvoCraft. Cardstock is by Leaving Prints. Journaling tags are printed on Astrobrites by Wausau Papers. Title font is Tuscarora. Journaling font is CK Journaling. Corner rounder punch is by Creative Memories.

Photos to find or request

- ❏ Photo of your child attending any extracurricular religious activities, like a youth group, Bible study or prayer group, etc.
- ❏ Photo of religious activities, like a chili supper, Vacation Bible School, or pageant
- ❏ Photo of your child at his or her baptism, bar mitzvah, bat mitzvah, confirmation or other milestone of faith
- ❏ Photo of your child preparing for or celebrating a religious holiday

Pictures to take

- ❏ Photo of his or her house of worship
- ❏ Photo of his or her pastor, priest, rabbi or children's minister
- ❏ Photo of service projects
- ❏ Photo of someone or something that represents "faith"
- ❏ Photo of the evidence of God's beauty in nature

A strong woman walks sure-footedly...but a woman of strength knows God will catch her when she falls...
A strong woman has faith that she is strong enough for the Journey...but a woman of strength has faith that it is in the journey that she will become strong...

—Unknown

To survive, we must begin to know sacredness.

—Chrystos

Passover-Charoset
by Rachel Wilson, age 6

This layout illustrates Rachel's key ingredients in preparing for Passover, a Jewish holiday. Her aunt cropped and matted the photos and Rachel listed the ingredients for making Charoset, one of the traditional foods eaten at the Seder meal.

Layouts about religious holidays become more meaningful when you include journaling about the preparations. Kids love telling what they like best about celebrations.

Supplies: Stickers are by Sandy Lion. Punch is by McGill. Journaling lines were drawn using a stencil from Journaling Genie. Hand lettering is by Rachel.

www.

Christian-based ideas for exploring your faith with children:
www.faith-at-home.com/
www.christianitytoday.c
om/parenting/features/
spiritual.html

Teaching about the Five Pillars of Islam:
www.teachingideas.co.uk/
re/fivepillars.htm

Spirituality for children:
www.susankramer.com/
spirituality.html

Christian-based lesson guides, crafts and activities:
www.sundayschoolcrafts.com

Buddhist meditations for kids:
www.idsl.net/heather/
onlinebuddhistcenter/
meditationhall/
meditationsforkids.html

Jewish early childhood educators' exchange:
www.geocities.com/
amynealw/

Spiritual writings, poems and quotes:
www.allspirit.co.uk/

Fruits of the Spirit
by Jessie Baldwin

Jessie copied dictionary page definitions and hymnal pages to use as journaling for this mini composition book. To give the pages more strength, she adhered patterned paper across a two-page spread of the book. To reduce extra bulk, she cut out several pages from the book and used these pages for the little papers in the vellum envelopes.

Supplies: Patterned paper is by 7Gypsies, Wordsworth and Karen Foster. Cardstock is by Bazzill Basics. Stickers are by Creative Imaginations, Me & My Big Ideas, K&Co., Jolee's Boutique and Flavia. Die cuts are by Rebecca Sower Freshcuts. Font on the Shrinky Dinks is DW Dingbats (www.twopeasinabucket.com). Stamp is by Hero Arts. Embellishments are from Jest Charming Embellishments and Making Memories.

My Confirmation
by Kaylin Spence, age 18

Pocket pages are a great way to hold a variety of odd-shaped memorabilia such as greeting cards. Kaylin wove paper strips to create her pocket and attached her journaling box on vellum strung through eyelets. What a perfect way to remember all of the people who wished her well.

SUPPLIES: Stencil is PC Blocky lettering template.

10: ALL ABOUT ME

This theme allows kids to spotlight their quirks and idiosyncrasies —likes, dislikes, pet peeves, "happy, shiny thoughts" — whatever can help them paint a picture of themselves as individuals.

When I sat down with my daughter to create her "Favorite Things" page, her first few answers came pouring out. Kids have little trouble thinking of things that make them happy.

Then, she faltered. So, I thought about time I had spent with her and what made me smile and say, "That's so Joanne!" Then I suggested some things to her. She lit up, and squealed, "Yeah! I do love that! Put that one down!"

Since Joanne is five years old, we take more of a team approach to her layouts. With my son, it was a matter of just suggesting a layout about a favorite thing. He took it from there.

This section describes how kids can record what sets them apart. It tells how to document things that appeal to them.

When I was in high school, I collected quotes. Just looking through my collection makes me smile. Sometimes one of those quotes brings to mind a certain person or event. One of the projects I chose for this chapter was a covered composition notebook (see page 71) for just such a collection.

My 20 Likes & Dislikes
by Rachel Yaceko, age 12

What a list of categories! Rachel was 12 when she made this layout. It will be interesting to see how her likes and dislikes change. It would also be interesting to create a page like this about each family member. Have your child conduct the interviews.

SUPPLIES: Patterned paper is by Paper Pizzazz. Vellum is by WorldWin Extraordinary Papers. Title and journaling font is Arial.

My 20 Likes and Dislikes

	Likes	Dislikes
1 - **Vegetable** - Corn		- Peas
2 - **Food** - Pizza / Chicken / potatos		- Liver
3 - **Soup** - Cheeseburger Soup		- French Onion Soup
4 - **Drink** - French Vanilla Coffee		- Milk
5 - **Fruit** - Apple / Pears / Kiwi		- Bananas
6 - **Snack** - Surprise Spread		- Cheezies
7 - **Bug** - Butterflies / Dragonflies		- Spiders
8 - **Animal** - Bears / Cats		- Skunks
9 - **Fish** - Dolphins		- Piranas
10 - **Music** - Pop Music		- Country / Blues
11 - **Color** - Blue / Pink		- Black
12 - **Movie** - A Walk to Rember		- Harry Potter
13 - **Book** - Any World War 2 book		- Red Rose ~ House of Tudor
14 - **Number** - 7 / $		- 6
15 - **Scrapbook tool** - punches		- 3-D embellishments
16 - **Season** - Spring / Summer		- Winter
17 - **Bird** - Hummingbirds		- Vulture
18 - **Flower** - Rose / Lilac		- Stink Weed
19 - **Road** - Paved		- Gravel
20 - **House** - Log Cabin / Victorian		- Igloo

I've never liked banana's (although I do like banana milkshakes and banana bread, etc...). I have been interested in World War II for a couple of years, and will read or watch just about anything to do with it! I wonder how my likes and dislikes will change as I grow older.....

You can also suggest that kids create layouts on other "free-association" type topics, like the Colors of My World layout by Misty and Mike Moats-Jones on page 70. They provided their associations for the colors red, blue, yellow and purple. Each color makes different people think of different things, so it's a different layout every time!

Layouts in this section can also allow kids to paint a picture of what kind of person they are. Typically when kids scrapbook, they like to do pages on events: birthdays, vacations, field trips and school functions. In this section, we're encouraging them to get a sense of who they are as a person.

We want them to scrap their youth while they are living it, as opposed to looking back on youth, as adults tend to do. Teen scrapper Erica Shaw thinks kids "have no problem getting themselves in their scrapbooks, but usually it's very 'on the surface.'" She suggests kids' layouts include "writing about their feelings more than 'this was when we all hung out at the mall.' Instead of writing about going to the mall, they could create a layout about why the friendships they have made are so important to them."

It's this emphasis that can show kids how unique they are—how they connect as an individual to their world.

Be Your Own Kind of Beautiful
by Barbara LeHoullier

Parenting girls through their teen years is a masterful art. In this layout, Barbara highlights her daughter's uniqueness and, in doing so, encourages her daughter to be true to herself.

The tags in this design work well to both include the captions as well as hold embellishments that illustrate the captions.

Supplies: Title font is A Yummy Apology. Fiber is by Adornments. Wire is by Artistic Wire.

Why is this theme important?

Encouraging kids to see themselves as individuals is sometimes challenging when so many kids simply want to fit in. Your role can be to emphasize that not only is okay to be unique, it's a good thing.

Many schools are implementing class content on character development and self-esteem issues because so many kids are floundering. You can compliment this approach by guiding children to put a positive spin on what they have to offer.

Focus on self-esteem along with their talents and gifts. This can feed into a strong sense of self-worth. Stress that they are wonderful, amazing and unique.

In my children's scrapbooks...

My daughter created pages about her favorite things, favorite people, and her "specialty dessert". My son did a layout on Harry Potter and plans to do pages on his card collections, being a picky eater and favorite jokes.

Prompts to trigger journaling

❑ What are your favorite—
  o Colors
  o Foods
  o Ways to relax
  o Creature comforts (include any recipes!)
  o Entertainment—movies, TV shows, books, music
  o Places

Colors of My World

by Misty Moates-Jones & Mike Moates, age 8

Misty and her son Mike created this layout at a Book of Me class I taught. I liked how they came up with the journaling together, both adding their thoughts to each square. Scrapbooking together is another way to include a child's perspective in a layout.

SUPPLIES: Cardstock is by Bazzill Basics. Title font is Bermuda Squiggle. Border punch is by Fiskars.

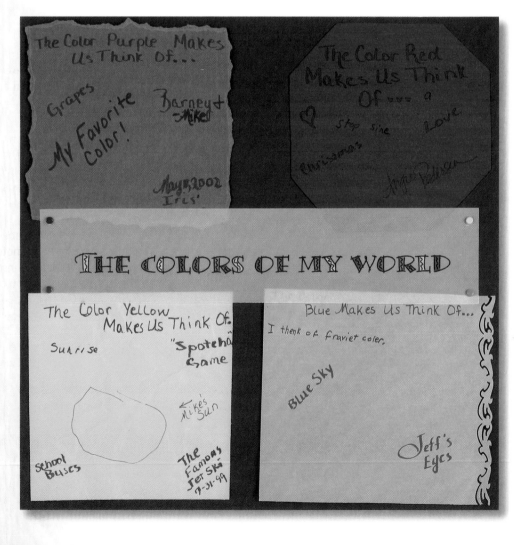

o Quotes

o Smells

o Memories

o People

o Vacation spots

o Things to do on a Saturday

o Things to do in the spring, summer, fall and winter

o Things to do with family or friends

o Things about your town

❑ If you could choose three things from your room that would describe you, what would they be?

❑ If you could take someone three places that describe your life, where would you take them?

❑ What five pieces of trivia about you do few people know?

❑ What one song can you count on to pick you up out of the dumps? What's your favorite "belt it out good and loud" song? Include the lyrics.

❑ If you had to choose five CDs to put on "random play" for a whole day, what would you choose? Why?

❑ Do a page on what makes you laugh. This could be a bullet-point list, a top 10 list, a photo or a collage of funny photos. Consider including names of movies, songs, actors, books and comic strips that are guaranteed to make you laugh.

It's good that we are all so different. It makes life more interesting.
—Unknown

I leave my portrait so that you will have my presence all the days and nights that I am away from you.
—Frida Kahlo

Against the assault of laughter nothing can stand.
—Mark Twain

Favorite Quotes Composition Notebook
by Angie Pedersen

A notebook like this is a great way to keep all of those snippets of ideas, quotations or lyrics in one place. Cover a regular composition notebook with cardstock or patterned paper and embellish as desired. This notebook is for collecting inspirational quotes but you could also use a similar book for responses to journaling prompts, favorite recipes, song lyrics or cute things your children say.

SUPPLIES: Patterned paper and die cuts are by Me & My Big Ideas. Black and white and red fibers are from friendly_fibers@yahoo.com. White eyelash fiber, heart brads, tags and transparency quote are from scrappys.net.

Joanne's Favorite Things

by Joanne Pedersen, age 5

To create this page, Joanne listed her favorite things with a little prompting from me. Then, she photographed her own pictures of some of these things. Later, she posed for a photo shoot wearing her favorite clothes and holding her favorite stuffed animals.

SUPPLIES: Cardstock and decorative edge scissors are by Fiskars. Stickers are by PSX Designs, SandyLion and Mrs. Grossman's. Punches are by Marvy and EK Success.

❑ What are the "signs of you"? What little things reveal that you live in your home? How are you leaving your mark? How would someone know, "Oh, she's been here!" Take some candid pictures, document them and scrap the page!

❑ List five things you're known for (recipes, clothing, sayings, etc.)

❑ Do a page on three to five embarrassing moments in your lifetime (consider using hidden journaling for this one).

❑ Create a layout about how lucky you are. What are your blessings?

❑ What are your three favorite places to shop? Consider chain stores, local traditions, or eclectic one-of-a-kind boutiques. What do you like best about each store? Describe some sensory impressions.

❑ What are 10 things you do every day, without fail?

❑ What are 10 lessons you've learned?

❑ List 10 things that tick you off.

❑ List five to 10 things you've done or said that you're proud of.

❑ What are five things in your purse or backpack that say something significant about you and your lifestyle?

❑ List the "ABCs of You"—think of a descriptive word for yourself, starting with each letter of the alphabet.

- What three things would you take with you if you were to be stranded on a desert island? You can only take one book, one music CD or cassette and one luxury item.
- Cover a composition notebook and use it to collect favorite quotes, song lyrics, recipes, etc.
- Do a page featuring you with different facial expressions. Title it "The Many Faces of Me."

Photos to find or request

- One good face shot—this can be used for several different layouts
- A photo of a messy room
- A photo of your child laughing
- A photo of your child amidst a collection
- Photos of your child with different facial expressions

Pictures to take

- A photo of his or her bookshelf
- A photo of favorite clothes
- Photos of "signs of you"
- A photo of something that makes him or her laugh
- A photo of favorite CDs, fanned out

The person who can bring the spirit of laughter into a room is indeed blessed.
—Bennett Cerf

At the height of laughter, the universe is flung into a kaleidoscope of new possibilities.
—Jean Houston

Laughter is the sensation of feeling good all over and showing it principally in one place.
—Josh Billings

With mirth and laughter let old wrinkles come.
—William Shakespeare

Pieces of Me
by Trista Jernigan, age 14

This is an adaptation of Jennifer Wohlenberg's layout featured in *The Book of Me.* Trista chose to cut her photo mosaic into diagonal, asymmetrical pieces and used creative lettering on her descriptive terms. This is a great layout for kids because they can usually come up with the seven to 10 words to describe themselves. It also captures their handwriting at the time.

SUPPLIES: Cardstock is by Serendipity and Hammermill. Hand lettering is by Trista.

Jo-Jo,
   My little Positive "Peanut", she is my quiet leader.
   Jo-Jo always thinks about other Peoples feelings before her own. I will always remember our homework Journey's together and our late nite snacks in bed. Jolene has a Perfect way of keeping her brothers in Line as well as being an "awesome" big & Little sister... not too many people can say they are right in the middle ... older brother/sisters as well as younger brothers/sisters. not to mention being an Aunt. Jolene has experienced Life from most angles that take People a lifetime to Live and done an awesome Job. I Love you and am Proud of You. Dad XOX

JoJo,
   How unique you are!! Even as a baby, you always were easy going no matter what. You are a very giving person & always thinking of others! I cant wait to see what you do in life... With your scrapbooking abilty - you will go far with it. I Love you with all my heart - stay unique youre so very special - MoM xox

Unique Jolene
by Jolene Belanger, age 14

There are two interesting things about this layout. Jolene included notes from each parent, describing how they think she is unique. Using other people's words helps add a different perspective to scrapbooks. Also, note how Jolene used little strips of patterned paper as a border on her portrait page and then repeated it on the notes page. This gives a sense of continuity to the layout.

SUPPLIES: Patterned paper is by Mustard Moon. Cardstock is by Serendipity Papers. Stencil is by Deja Views. Hand lettering is by Jolene and her parents.

Things You May Not Know About Me
by Hannah Jezak, 13

This was the first layout that Hannah ever made! The journaling was computer generated—Hannah said that she enjoyed picking out fonts, colors and pictures. It is a wonderful conversation starter to ask children what five to seven things most people don't know about them.

Supplies: Fonts are MT Curlz, ITC Snap, Andy, ITC Kristen, ITC Tempus Sans, Parade, Lucida Handwriting and Ink Pen 2 Script. Deckle Edge Scissors are by Fiskars.

WWW.

Find the lyrics to your favorite song:
www.azlyrics.com

All About Me unit for the classroom:
www.kinderkorner.com/me.html

Describe (and scrap!) your personal treasures:
www.canteach.ca/elementary/personal2.html
www.canteach.ca/elementary/personal4.html

Write a poem about yourself:
www.canteach.ca/elementary/poetry3.html
www.tlsbooks.com/alphabetpoem.htm

Create your own trading card (and include it on a layout!):
www.eduplace.com/activity/tradecard.html

ABCs of Me activity:
www.scrapyourstories.com/abcs-of-me.htm

List 100 things you love:
www.scrapyourstories.com/easyas1-2-100.htm

Covering a composition notebook:
www.jordanpaperarts.com/article401.htm
www.scrapnsafari.com/e10journals.htm

Storybook Project

The Coat of a Thousand Furs
by Christina Foran

Of all of the stories that Christina has written, this is her favorite so far. She brought it to life using watercolors and let the bookmarks tell the story. Torn edges and gold stamping gives the layout a storybook look. This idea could be modified to scrapbook a major event like a trip or a summer program.

SUPPLIES: Cardstock is by Awasau and Crown. Suede paper is by SEI. Fonts are Edda, Carpenter ICG, Book Antiqua, Chase Callas SH. Stamps are by Inkadinkadoo. Gold ink is by Anna Griffin.

2

before her very eyes, the princess' fair skin grew dark and [roug]h. Her nails grew sharp and fangs protruded from her soft [fles]h. Her nose curled and her body was transformed. The fur of [her] coat took root and covered her fully. She cried out, but only [a] monstrous strain escaped.

As soon as her attendants heard the frightening noise, they [r]ushed into the house. There they found only the cackling, old woman and a hideous beast.

"Where is the princess?" they demanded. The old woman only laughed at them for a moment and vanished the next.

Believing, the beast had devoured their fair princess, they threw chains around its neck and drug it into the dungeon, deep within the king's castle. The princess knew that resistance be fruitless.

From her cage the next morning, she heard the sound of sorrowful stringed instruments. All the country mourned the death of the young princess, but because of its magical coat no one could bring themselves to slay the beast they thought responsible.

She passed many years in that dark dungeon alone, remembering her family and the joyful days she had spent in this very castle. Most men forget about the beast which lurked in their dungeon. Its existence was reduced from gossip to rumors and from rumors to fable.

One day a young man, an apprentice to the royal guard, was given responsibilities in the dungeon. Twice a day he was to deliver meals to the prisoners. The other guards warned him about the mythical beast.

"Be careful, tonight, not to get too close to the slot when you slip some supper into the seventeenth cell," one guard called after him.

The apprentice turned and asked, "Why's that?"

"Folks say a terrible beast haunts that cell," another jeered.

"I'm not scared," he defended firmly.

"Well, ya should be!" barked an older guard. "That beast could tear a boy like you limb from limb."

The boy jumped and the company fell into laughter, whooping and hollering and slapping their knees. When the apprentice turned away to continue his work, his face turned red with anger and embarrassment.

That night he paused at the seventeenth cell. All lay still. The cell seemed empty. The slot opened with a creak and a clank, and the boy set the dinner bowl into the cell. Nothing stirred. The dark cell remained silent. Yet, morning, the morning, the apprentice collected the empty bowls.

2

5

At the next new moon the king held a banquet. Again, the prison guard left his keys with the apprentice. Again, the young man found a candle, and also a brush, and crept carefully down the corridor to the seventeenth cell. The keys clattered in the lock as he opened the heavy, steel door. This time, though, the beast sat waiting by the door for him.

The boy patted its head, and the beast panted happily. "Guess what I've brought," he said and pulled out the brush from his coat. The beast thumped its tail, and the boy began combing out the mud that had become matted into the beast's coat.

The beast began the purr ferociously. "Never heard a beast purr like that before. S'pose it means you're enjoying this, eh?"

For an hour he brushed and combed all the dirt and tangles out of the beast's thick coat. With a sigh he finally stepped back to admire his work. *Why, the fur shines like the night sky.* The sight set him dreaming. When he came to, he found those emerald eyes staring back at him.

"There's something odd about you. You must be some sort of magical creature. I don't believe you're actually what you seem to be." He watched those emerald eyes dance as he spoke. He almost drifted off into wonder again when the beast stirred suddenly.

"What is it?" As he said the words, the smell of smoke tickled his lungs. "Fire?" He rose and ran to the door. Peaking out, he saw flames leaping down the stairs. The other guards had evacuated, and soon the room filled with smoke. The young man coughed violently and started to faint. At once the beast caught him and hid him within its coat.

The beast leaped through the flames and bounded up the stairs. Outside she laid her friend under an old fir, the same she played under as a child. She nudged his face, but he lay breathless.

5

3

On the night that the king threw another of his grand balls, the prison guard left his keys to the apprentice and snuck upstairs to catch a bit of the excitement. The guard had given him his chance, the chance to face whatever was locked in the seventeenth cell and the chance to prove his courage to the others. He found a candle and made his way down the corridor.

"Beast!" he called outside the cell. He heard no reply. The keys clattered in the lock as he opened the heavy steel door. He could see nothing in the dark cell. As he shined his light around the room, he heard a low howl. His candle guided him to the darkest corner of the cell. Indeed, huddled in that corner hid a monstrous thing. Yet, the boy could only stare in wonder at the sight of its amazing coat. *I can't tell exactly what it should be, for it has the fur of a thousand different animals.*

He set his candle on the floor and crouched down to look into the face of the beast. It lifted its head, and the boy recoiled at the sight. The beast buried its face again and edged closer into the corner. It began to shake and moan.

The young man recovered quickly and placed the palm of his hand on the beast's heaving shoulder. *Why, it's as soft as snow!* He thought, and he quickly apologized.

"Forgive me, Beast. I judged too hastily. I came to visit you. You don't need to be afraid. Come now, don't cry."

The beast lifted its wet face. Its appearance didn't startle the boy as badly now. It sat and stared at him with its emerald eyes.

3

4

"There, now, that's better," the young man coaxed. For the first time he fully noticed the beast's long fangs and sharp claws, yet he didn't fear them. He also noticed how dirty and tangled the beautiful coat had become.

"You know, you should take better care of your handsome coat. Next time I'll—" He stopped suddenly, for he heard footstep on the stairs. The bang of the heavy door echoed throughout the dark cell as it closed. He slipped the key inside the lock and out again. Then he ran to meet the prison guard and inquire about the ball. The guard, however, had returned drunk and could only rave all night about the beautiful Duchess of York (who incidentally never made it to the ball that night).

The next morning, the apprentice tip-toed quietly to the seventeenth cell with breakfast for the beast. He peaked through the slot and found those emerald eyes staring back at him. For a moment he forgot that a beast sat on the other side of the door.

"Morning, Beast," the young man greeted and slipped the breakfast bowl through the slot. He felt the swish of a tail and heard steps going to and fro. The beast pawed the slot with its large, monstrous hand in greeting.

The apprentice felt the glances of the other guard and whispered, "Farewell for now, Beast."

4

6

She roared in anger. The noises of battle filled her ears. The castle was under attack. The captain of the king's army sounded the call for a last defense. She must not fear them now.

The beast raced toward the battle with a piercing roar. With one swipe of her paw she crushed ten men. With her sharp fangs, she devoured another dozen. Within minutes half of the enemy's army had been defeated. The rest retreated, but the beast pursued them.

As she raised her paw to smite the last of the enemy's army, she felt a sword at her throat. She turned to find the evil queen smirking at the opposite end of the blade. Her cowardly soldiers fled anon.

"We meet again... m'lady," the queen began. "I figured you'd be dead by now or banished." She cackled and looked fiercely into the eyes of the beast. "You've caused me a great deal of trouble, you know." She looked around. Her army lay obliterated. "A great deal, indeed! Well, I shall make sure that it will never happen again."

As she prepared a blow, an arrow whizzed through the air and penetrated her heart straight through. The sword fell from the hands of the evil queen, and with her dying breath the beast began to tremble. The princess' skin grew fair again. Her nose uncurled and her body was transformed. The coat came unclasped and slipped off her weary shoulders.

"Beast!" She heard the cry and saw a young man running towards her bow in hand. She recognized her friend from the dungeon. He cried out again, but as soon as he saw the beautiful princess he fell to his knees.

"Forgive me, your highness. I judged too hastily."

The princess lowered her gaze but said nothing. The young man saw the mysterious coat lying on the ground and looked up, astonished. He found those emerald eyes staring back at him.

"It *is* you!"

The princess smiled and reached out her hand. The young man took it. It felt as soft as snow. He rose, but would not let go of the princess' fair hand.

"Thank you," spoke the princess.

"No, your highness, I should be thanking you. You saved my life. You saved the whole kingdom."

"Yes, but you saved *my* life. Twice."

A horn blew in the distance and the captain of the king's army came riding towards them. "Have you seen?—Oh, your highness, Princess!" he cried in unbelief. "How?—Oh, your highness, you must come quickly to the castle. The king lies dying."

6

Scrapping with Young Children

Here are some tips on scrapbooking with young children, based on my experiences with my six-year-old daughter Joanne.

Set aside time to scrap. Expect to work on just their pages at the beginning. This saves you frustration when you don't get anything done on your own pages!

Choose photos. From your duplicate pictures, let your child pick which photos to scrap. Or suggest a particular topic and let them pick the photos.

Choose paper. Looking at the photos they've chosen, suggest two to three solid colors for background paper. Once that's chosen, offer a selection of a few patterned papers. This gives kids the "power of personal choice", while you also maintain a little power over your own supplies!

Crop or shape your photos. Discuss cropping to make sure just what they want is the photo ("Do you want that part of the room in your picture, or do you want to cut it out?"). My daughter can use my trimmer and I do any cutting that needs an Exacto knife. Whenever possible, I want her to practice her fine-motor skills.

Mat the photos. If your child would like to mat the photos, you can ask which paper she would like to mat the photo on, position it on the paper, then either let the child trim it to size or you do it. My personal choice is to let your child do as much as possible.

Journal the story. Ask leading questions and journal it using their words. By leading questions, I mean:

o What did you like best?
o What do you remember most?
o Who was with you?
o Where did you go?
o What did you do there?

Journaling can be in your handwriting, in theirs or on the computer. I handwrite the journaling on a separate piece of cardstock so it becomes another element for my daughter to place on the layout.

Adhere all the pieces. Once the photos are cropped and matted, and the journaling done, hand your child all the pieces and let them place them on the background however they like. Yes, they're typically not straight (either in cut or placement) or with any adult sense of balance—but it's their page. Let them do the adhesive (under your watchful eye).

Admire the finished project. Read the journaling back to them again -- kids always love hearing stories, especially when it's their own!

Groups of kids. Instead of a one-on-one scrapping session, break the kids up into smaller groups. When I taught five year olds in preschool, and we had an ambitious activity, like painting T-shirts, we would do the activity during center time. One of the centers was the T-shirts (other centers would be manipulatives, reading, kitchen, etc). So while most of the class was occupied elsewhere, we could take however many to give a little more hands-on attention.

One adult can probably take up to five children at a time While you're taking journaling dictation for one student, the others could be cropping, matting or adhering. Do not attempt to lead large groups by yourself. Some children need more help with cutting or other tasks and normal disruptions make it too difficult to help everyone.

INDEX

It's Not the End, It's the Beginning!

Register for one of Angie's bulletin boards online at www.onescrappysite.com:

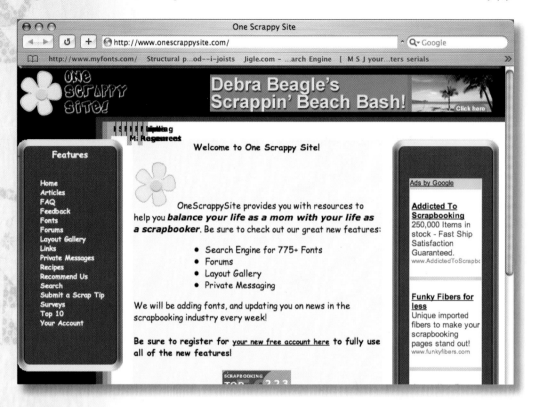

Click on the "forums" button in the lefthand menu and register to join other scrapbookers, parents and teachers.